Web Operations Dashboards, Monitoring, and Alerting

An introduction to cloud monitoring and alerting

Web Operations Dashboards, Monitoring, and Alerting
An introduction to cloud monitoring and alerting

www.stevefenton.co.uk

Cover Image: John Snow's chart overlaying clusters of cholera cases on a map of Soho, London. The chart was created in 1854, and published in On the Mode of Communication of Cholera. This map was used to change the prevalent beliefs about disease transmission, and indicates the cause of the cholera epidemic: a water pump on the corner of Broad Street and Cambridge Street. The pump was supplying contaminated water, and removing the handle of the pump saved lives.
The image is public domain.

For Rebecca and Lily

Contents

Introduction

In 1854 Soho, London was hit by a major outbreak of cholera. In three days, 127 people in the area had died and this total would rise to 616 people before the outbreak was over.

The prevalent theory at the time was that the air was contaminated with a miasma that carried the disease from decaying organic matter through the air, infecting individuals who were unlucky enough to breathe in the particles.

John Snow's Chart – Clusters shown as black bars

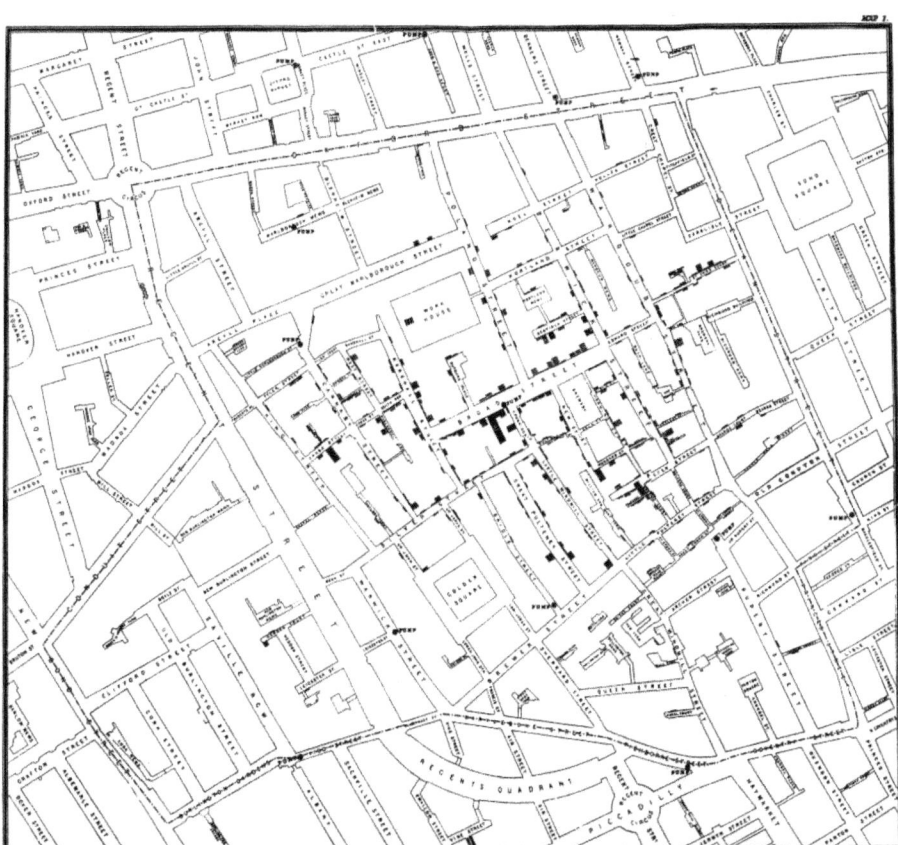

However, John Snow did not subscribe to this theory and to convince others of his observation that it was contaminated water causing the epidemic, Snow put together a map of Soho overlaid with clusters of cholera instances. This demonstrated that the cases were clustered around a water pump on the corner of Broad Street and Cambridge Street.

With this data, compiled into this chart, Snow could demonstrate that London had been split into two populations, one that was exposed to contamination, and one that was not.

Snow's theory went that if you received your water supply from the Southwark and Vauxhall Company, or from the Lambeth Water Company, you were being exposed to water contaminated with cholera. If you took your supply from the New River Company or the Chelsea Company your water was cleaner.

Snow's theory was further proven by showing that instances of cholera stopped in several prisons just days after changing their water supply.

Map of Water Company Supplies

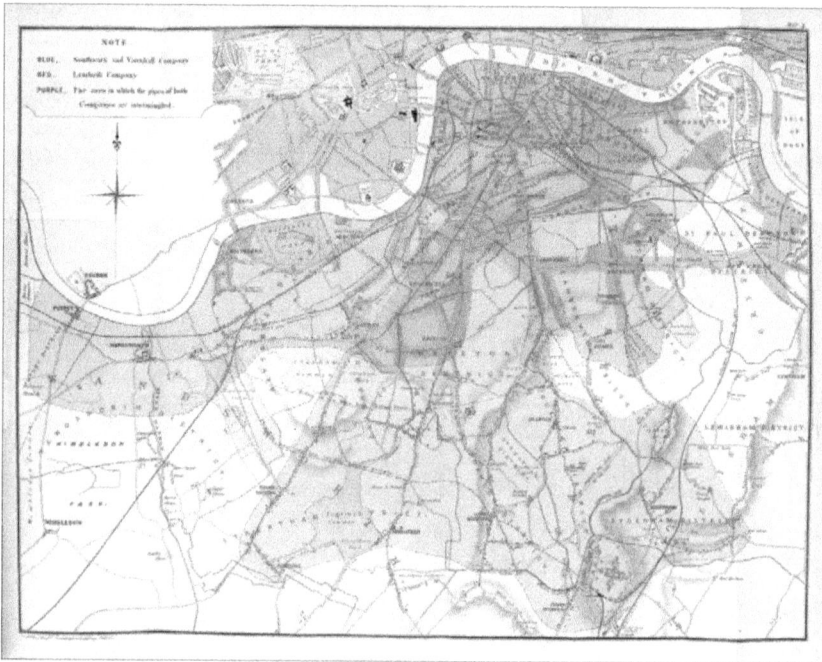

Snow described how the tragedy had uncovered information that the grandest experiment could not have found.

See www.ph.ucla.edu/epi/snow/snowbook3.html.

No fewer than three hundred thousand people of both sexes, of every age and occupation, and of every rank and station, from gentlefolks down to the very poor, were divided into two groups without their choice, and, in most cases, without their knowledge; one group being supplied water containing the sewage of London, and amongst it, whatever might have come from the cholera patients, the other group having water quite free from such impurity.

Compiling the cholera chart in the Victorian era took a great deal of effort. If this information had been available instantly, how many more lives might have been saved?

Now your web operations story probably doesn't involve a life or death situation for three-hundred thousand Victorian Londoners – but the link between crisis management and data collection and visualisation is just as applicable to your next outage.

John Snow has provided an inspirational real-world example that sets the context for this book. When things go wrong, it takes someone calm, professional, and disciplined to set it right. Someone who can fly in the face of conventional thinking and make up their own mind. Someone who can rise to the occasion and solve a problem when nobody else can. That someone is you!

Who This Book is For

This book is for anyone involved in software development who needs some practical tips to kick off their web operations monitoring journey. I have implemented the techniques and strategies in this book while taking care of web operations for an organisation providing a suite of web applications to a blue-chip multinational automaker.

Before I began this work, I already knew a lot about web operations because I had worked with some smart engineers in previous jobs, but when it came to the task of tackling web operations monitoring I realised I had a lot of practical questions for which I struggled to find straightforward answers.

I had questions such as "What should I add to my dashboards?", "When should I use different chart types?", and "When should I step up to red alert?"

Which means changing the bulb
www.youtube.com/watch?v=81W8tG3wH_4.

I needed to know where to start, and how to evolve a "web operations monitoring strategy" from scratch. Time and again the answer I obtained was simply:

It Depends

So, if you are wondering which metrics are important, confused about the kind of chart you should add to your dashboards, or want to discover how to find and fix incidents before your customers even know there is a problem; this book can fill those gaps in just a couple of commutes. I'll explain what metrics to start with, and how you can use a simple process to refine your strategy over time to find metrics that are appropriate to your context.

What is in This Book?

This book covers the following web operations monitoring fundamentals:

- Incident management
- Metric collection
- Creating dashboards
- Selecting metrics
- Choosing chart types
- Monitoring metrics to detect problems
- Raising alarms and sending alerts

All the examples I have used are based on Datadog, although a tremendous belt-full of other tool options is available. Much of the information in this book applies across the board no matter which tools you select. The monitoring platform marketplace is highly competitive, so the tool vendors are constantly adding new features.

Don't get lost down the rabbit-hole of feature lists and comparison matrices though; decide which features are core to your web operations strategy and select a tool that is rock solid in those areas. Until you build up a substantial history of data you aren't committed to a tool; so, pick one for now and change your mind when you have collected more information using the advice scattered throughout the book.

What isn't in this Book?

I am zooming in on web operations monitoring in this book; that means programming, builds, testing, deployment, and configuration are all out. So is infrastructure as code and application performance management. There is a chapter that quickly summarises tools in these areas, and you can broaden your knowledge into these areas once you've got your monitoring under control.

I'm also not going to give you every single instruction you need to install and configure Datadog. If you are looking at implementing web operations monitoring, I know you are smart. If I write step-by-step instructions I think you'll find me patronising. Instead, I will point you in the right direction and let you follow along without me telling you to "click on the Dashboards link in the main menu and press the third button on the left, titled 'Edit'".

Self-Indulgent Introduction

If you are wondering why you should listen to a stranger on the Internet on such an important topic as web operations monitoring, you may find it useful to know a little about my background and how I ended up being involved in this subject.

In the words of my excellent ex-boss I am: "... a top-class developer - but this is just the start. His stand out skills lie in coaching and inspiring developers in software craftsmanship and being agile. He's a great motivator, great tutor and excellent professional. Thoroughly recommended to any development team". And an ex-colleague said: "Working with Steve over the past couple of years has been a great experience. He possesses huge knowledge in all aspects of software development and shows great passion when it comes to protecting Agile and Lean principles, which he has mentored and taught the team a great deal about. He is also a fantastic software developer from a technical point of view, the code he writes (whatever the language) always has had a lot of care taken over it and it shows - it is invariably clean, readable, adaptable and designed beautifully!"

I pulled these recommendations from my LinkedIn profile not just to impress you, but because I want you to know you are in safe hands.

You can view my profile here: www.linkedin.com/in/stevefenton/.

I cut my teeth on web operations as part of installing DevOps from scratch for an organisation. They had many web applications and services hosted on an even greater number of servers. As part of the process of "automating all the things" (including builds, tests, and deployment automation with Octopus Deploy) I discovered that there was no real web operations picture in the organisation, and firefighting mode was dialled up to eleven.

Eleven? See en.wikipedia.org/wiki/Up_to_eleven.

The Psychology of Web Operations

A typical incident in an organisation without web operations starts with one of your customers contacting you to say they can't access a system. This will almost certainly be an important customer, because they are more engaged with your software. It may also be the trickle that precedes the flood as the phone lines start lighting up.

When the pressure is on, the human consciousness goes myopic. The scattergun is un-holstered and deployed liberally. After some time, and with a bit of luck, things start to work. As soon as things are working, the focus shifts back to the day job and everyone forgets what went wrong and what changes were made during the panic. Conversations after the fact will focus on the heroic response to the fault and on the narrative fallacy that explains how the problem was unavoidable.

The type of environment that promotes heroism is self-perpetuating, because nothing is learned from incidents, which means the same failures will happen again.

A long time ago, I was on standby for an overnight release of a piece of critical business software. The release had gone wrong and I witnessed some very strange behaviour that shaped my thinking about responding to failure.

The programmer investigating the failed release had started to install programming tools on the target server with the intention of writing an application that would diagnose the problem. Installing a programming IDE is not a quick task, and writing a program from scratch that detects what has gone wrong with a complex deployment is not exactly a simple task either. Several "co-pilots" tried to convince the programmer to step back and consider the options, but were waved away by the "captain", who had developed tunnel vision that prevented any information not related to writing a new application from getting through.

I petitioned the release manager to clear the decks and allow one of the other "co-pilots" and me to investigate the cause of the deployment failure. Our approach was far less heroic. We picked up the deployment checklist and worked through it step-by-step to validate that the steps had been completed correctly:

1. Put the application in maintenance mode. **Check**.
2. Back up the database. **Check**.
3. Execute the database upgrade scripts. **Check**.
4. Run the installer. **Fail**.

The "Run the Installer" item was in position 22 on the checklist. I shortened the list for brevity.

The deployment had failed because the step of running the installer had been missed. This was the easiest deployment problem to fix. Ever. The installer file was sat waiting to be run. We ran it, and the release was successful.

So what causes people to do crazy and dangerous things when they react to an incident? According to Malcolm Gladwell, there are two error-modes that cause this: choking, and panic. It is useful to understand these two modes.

Based on Malcolm Gladwell, What the Dog Saw (and other adventures). Penguin Books. 2009.

To illustrate, there are three diagrams below. The first is the calm mode, which illustrates how we operate when we can access all our faculties. This is followed by diagrams for the panic mode and choking mode.

Let's begin with the healthy, calm, and professional mode of response to a crisis. It has instinct and intuition on one side, and explicit and implicit learning on the other. This response mode is partly down to temperament, and partly attributable to experience.

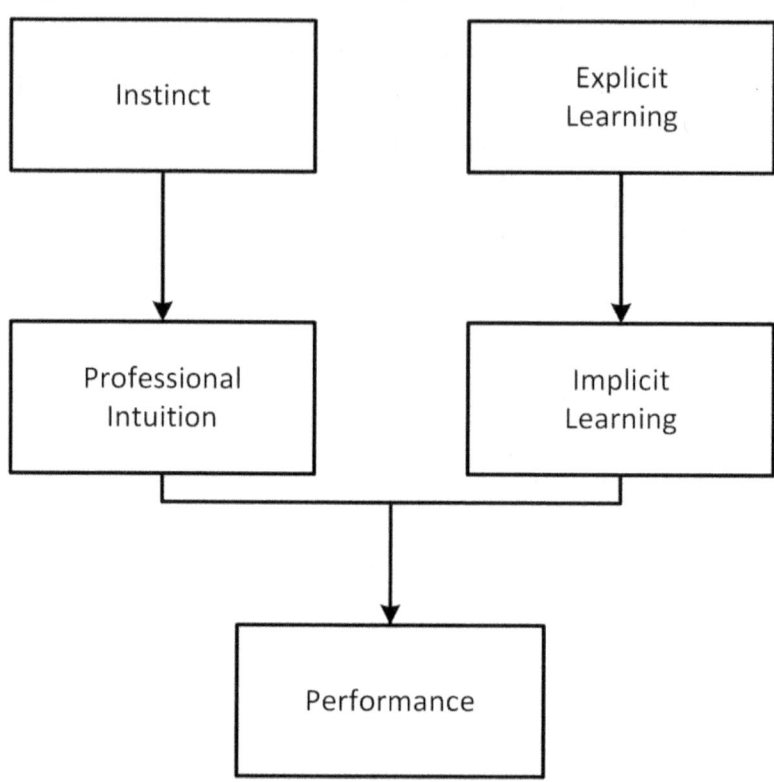

In contrast to the calm mode shown above, panic mode causes us problems accessing our learning. On top of this our professional intuition is hampered. This means we act instinctively, either performing seemingly random acts, or freezing entirely. Tunnel-vision descends and we can become entirely focussed on a single detail, ignoring all the other information that is available.

Panic mode is illustrated in the diagram that follows.

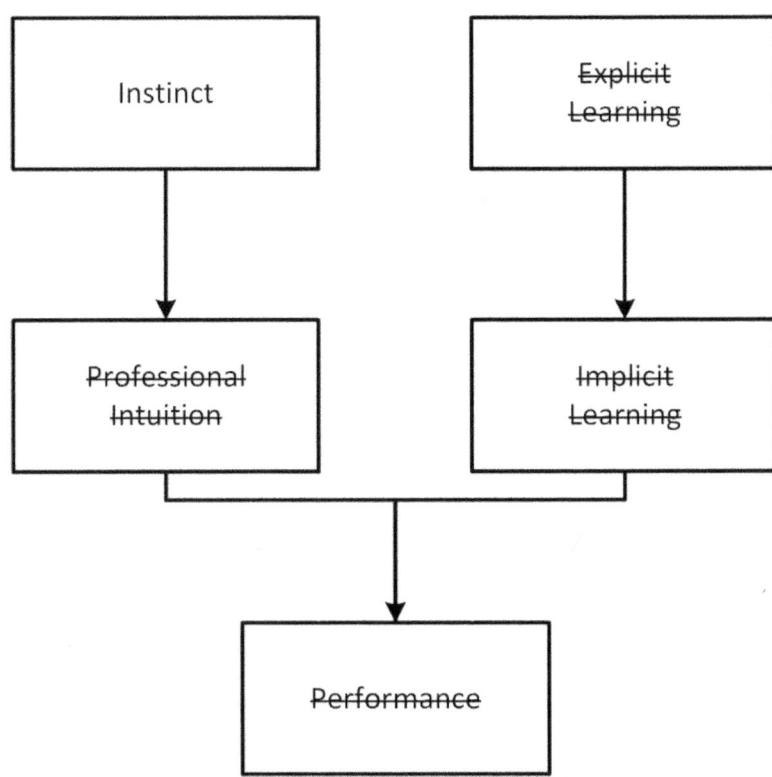

While panic mode affects the right-hand side of the diagram more, choking has more effect on the left-hand side.

When we choke, we fall back on our explicit learning. Everything becomes mechanical and clunky. We lose access to our instinct and intuition, and all the fluid and effortless actions encoded in our implicit learning.

Choking mode is shown on the next page.

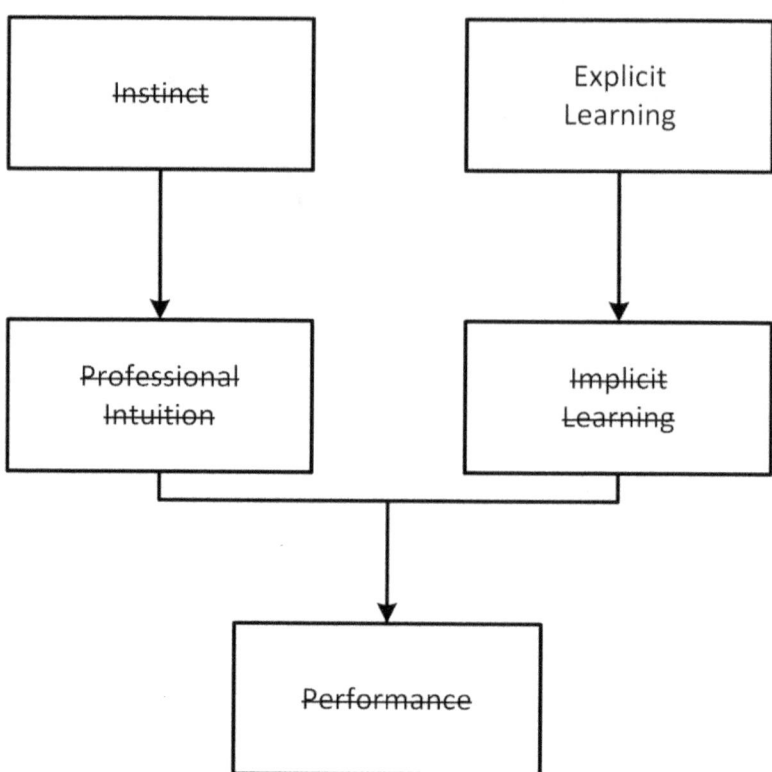

Both choking and panic will negatively impact performance in a crisis. When a bad incident is made much worse by the response, choking and panic are almost certainly at play.

If you have a disposition for either panic mode or choking mode, you may want to ensure that someone else has the controls during an incident. That doesn't mean you can't play a part in web operations; you'll find plenty of other areas to add value throughout this book.

Introducing Web Operations

With the help of a smart and talented team, I introduced an incident management process, set up a monitoring platform, and encouraged the use of failures as a learning opportunity.

I won't lie, things got worse before they got better. When you make the health of your application and infrastructure visible, you will find out about problems that have gone undetected for a long time. The thing is, they are still problems whether you know about them or not; and you can't shoot down problems until you can see them.

It didn't take long, though, for the conflagration-style perpetual state of emergency to be displaced by calm and professional incident management. Faults were fixed before they impacted customers. Improvements were made to the architecture and to the software. The product smoothly expanded into multiple datacentres serving customers around the world.

I know that you want to arrive at this utopian destination; it has five-star reviews on Trip Advisor and there are free fruit mocktails by the pool. So, stick with me and I'll help you to plot a similar course to web operations bliss. Things will still break sometimes (because if Azure and AWS can fail, so can you), but as you'll find out; how you respond in a crisis, and how the business reacts to your response, can be entirely transformed.

What is Web Operations Monitoring?

If we take the whole task of software development and slice it down, we can carve out a part that is called DevOps, which is unsurprisingly a clipped compound of "Development" and "Operations". If we slice again, we can lop off a chunk that we'll call web operations. Another cut will give us monitoring, which is core to success in the other areas.

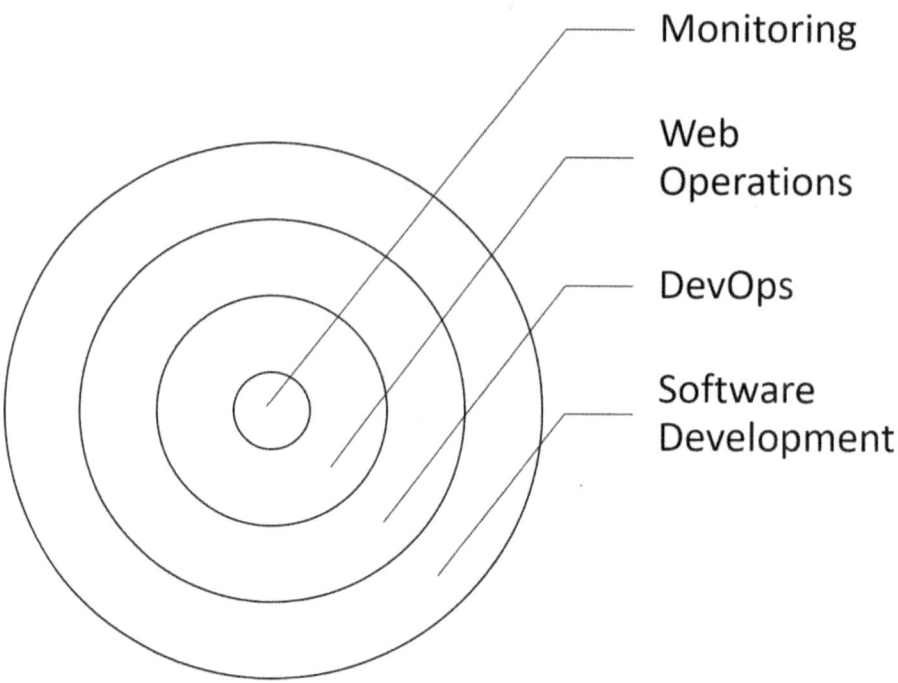

Monitoring

Web
Operations

DevOps

Software
Development

That's enough with the apple metaphor. Let's start cutting...

Side note! Although DevOps is quickly becoming the de-facto environment for web operations, this book covers material that works in any set up, in any company. Whether you are part of a self-organising team or locked in a dedicated operations war room, if you have web applications that must be available to users and customers, you will benefit from the topics covered in this book. I'm sure you'll manage to squeeze the content that is contextualised with DevOps into whatever shape suits your current organisation.

DevOps

The term DevOps refers to a collaborative software development and delivery process that aligns to agile software development. The aim of DevOps is to increase the speed, frequency, and reliability of making and releasing software. DevOps bundles together tools, roles, process, practices, and most importantly: an entire developer culture.

You can view the Agile Manifesto at agilemanifesto.org.

Loosely speaking, DevOps covers the following cross-functional areas:

1. Code
2. Build
3. Test
4. Package
5. Release
6. Configure
7. Monitor

The tools of DevOps can slot into one of more of these areas. While a tool may cross multiple areas, there is no single tool that can do everything. Being able to snap tools in and out of your toolchain allows you to select the best tools for critical areas, even if you make do with average tools elsewhere. Monitoring is a critical area.

Here is an example toolchain, showing a sample of actual tools in use within an imaginary DevOps team. This is just one illustrative set up out of a mind-boggling number of possible tool choices and combinations.

1. **Code**: Visual Studio Team Services for development, code reviews, source control, and merging

2. **Build**: Visual Studio Team Services for continuous integration and automated builds

3. **Test**: Visual Studio Team Services to run unit and integration tests during the build

4. **Package**: Octopack to create packages, which are then stored in a library by Octopus Deploy

5. **Release**: Octopus Deploy to release software and handle approvals, deployment automation, and the deployment pipeline

6. **Configure**: Octopus Deploy to handle configuration of the software, Desired State Configuration to handle infrastructure as code

7. **Monitor**: Datadog to monitor the software and for application performance management

You can easily switch out any of the specific tools mentioned here for one of the other alternatives. Part of the beauty of DevOps is that you can create the right combination for your specific team.

DevOps may be a term that has been coined recently, but it represents something of a renaissance. Just as Kent Beck re-discovered test-driven development, DevOps has unearthed the ancient practice of a single team taking care of the whole process of software development.

On 9th September 1947, the Harvard technical team working on the Mark II were running a DevOps culture. A cross-functional team of engineers fixed Relay #70 in Panel F by removing a dead moth, allowing Grace Hopper (one of the first four computer programmers in the world) to make her famous comment about the "*First actual case of a bug being found*". There was an outage between 3:45 PM and 4:30 PM due to this fault.

Good software development practices are not new. The kind of smart people that created computers, programming languages, and compilers also maintained (literal) log files, created automated tests, deployed their own code, and fixed it when there was a fault.

If you want to learn more about DevOps, Mike Loukides has written a great summary here radar.oreilly.com/2012/06/what-is-devops.html.

Wikipedia has a good signpost page that points to many useful articles here en.wikipedia.org/wiki/DevOps.

Web Operations

Within DevOps, the role of web operations is concerned with the last three boxes in our DevOps diagram: release, configure, and monitor. If you aren't working in a DevOps culture, this diagram may still be a fairly accurate visualisation of where web operations fit into the picture. No matter how your organisation is designed, collaboration with the roles working to your left is essential to success.

1. ~~Code~~
2. ~~Build~~
3. ~~Test~~
4. ~~Package~~
5. **Release**
6. **Configure**
7. **Monitor**

The web operations role is responsible for keeping web applications healthy. That includes the software, platforms, and infrastructure that make up the application as well as all those that the application relies on. A web operations engineer can perform many tasks relating to the health of the application from ensuring releases don't disrupt service, to responding to sudden spikes in traffic, to handling problems caused by hardware faults.

Because the combination of factors is so complex, it is not possible to predict what might happen tomorrow; and this variability is what will attract or repel people to the web operations role.

There are five stages of web operations that track the journey from survival and constant firefighting right the way through to a calm and disciplined profession – and you can expect to see many colours of craziness if you are taking an organisation along this road. You'll need to be cool in a crisis to handle this work without harming your own health.

Web Operations Monitoring

We have finally arrived at our definition of web operations monitoring. This is what the book is all about. The monitoring part of web operations is often thought to be software tool. This is only part of the story though. There are three key tools in your web operations monitoring and two of them are not software:

1. A culture of learning
2. A solid incident management process
3. A monitoring platform

The chapter on Incident Management covers the learning culture and incident management process in some detail. If you can't wait for the colourful charts and audible alarms, don't worry; this book contains plenty of those too.

DevOps Tools Part I

The DevOps tools have been sliced into two parts to create a veritable fly-by of hardware you can stuff into your utility-belt. In this first part, I will briefly summarize the key tools that are in keeping with the main theme of this book. In the next part, we'll cover all the other stuff to complete the picture; but they won't get mentioned again afterwards. Or to put it another way:

- This chapter is a teaser for the rest of the book

- The next chapter will give you some ideas about what to look at later

The foundational aspects of web operations monitoring are incident management, event log aggregation, metric collection, dashboards, monitoring, and alerting. Many of these are provided by a solid monitoring platform and it is becoming increasingly common for this monitoring platform to be hosted in the cloud. With fewer organisations hosting everything in one place (or even with one supplier) – and even fewer people wanting to look after the large volumes of data and data crunching on their own infrastructure, cloud monitoring platforms are certainly in high demand. Because of this, there are many high-quality options to choose from.

Asides from incident management, which is going to be down to you, any good monitoring platform will supply all the tools you need for monitoring and alerting. You will almost certainly want application performance management later too. Here is a quick summary of the various tools we're going to dive into.

Incident Management

This is the very first tool you need to add to your utility belt. It is vital to have an incident management process that provides a checklist of how to handle a fault and that encourages a blameless black-box investigation into the causes of the failure. The incident management process will describe who participates in an incident, and what steps should be followed to ensure an already bad problem isn't upgraded to a total disaster.

Event Log Aggregation

Event log aggregation is a fundamental part of log management. By forwarding logs from individual servers to a central source, not only can you get an overview of errors logged across your whole infrastructure in one place; you can also discard the uploaded events from the individual hosts, saving you disk space. You can also search the aggregated events and find patterns of logs that might not be apparent on individual hosts.

Metric Collection

Metric collection involves snapshotting certain information about the state of the application and infrastructure, and forwarding that representation of the state to the monitoring platform. This may be basic utilisation metrics, such as disk space utilisation, CPU state, memory consumed, or metrics based on integrations with databases and web servers. You can also forward metrics directly from your application to use as part of your monitoring strategy.

Dashboards

A dashboard is a visual collection of information that can be used to understand the health of your infrastructure and services. A good dashboard immediately reveals whether things are healthy or in need of attention. Dashboards are also vital for incident management, helping you to detect anomalies, correlate metrics, and discover the root cause of any fault.

Monitoring

The monitoring process continually trawls the metrics and can be used to raise alarms based on fixed thresholds, the size of changes, or algorithms that detect unusual behaviour. Over time, you will fine tune your list of monitors, and their conditions so you find out about problems and fix them before they impact your customers (or your bank balance). Monitoring is continuous and thousands of metrics will be checked every minute to confirm everything is working.

Alerting

Alerting has two components, an alarm that detects that the conditions of a monitor are breached, and one or more alerts that tell humans about the problem. Each alert is usually raised via multiple routes, for example email, text message, and smartphone app. Using multiple routes helps to ensure that the message makes it through. When relying on email for alerts, your critical notifications must compete within a noisy inbox, where messages may not be timely and are typically checked in batches; also, you'll never find out about your mail server failing.

The strict definition of alarm and alert is not followed with much discipline, so expect to find alarms called alerts, alerts called alarms, and other semantic silt. I'm certainly guilty of using the terms interchangeably; as do many of the tools.

DevOps Tools Part II

The tools in this chapter are either not directly related to monitoring, or are advanced topics that are best delayed until you have a firm grasp of the tools in the previous chapter, which is the case with Application Performance Management.

Automated Builds

Code should be checked into source control multiple times every day. Every time code is committed to source control, the code should be compiled and tested. This ensures that the software is always in a releasable state and will mean errors are detected sooner, when they are easier and cheaper to fix. This is a process called continuous integration, which is a key part of DevOps.

Read more about continuous integration here www.thoughtworks.com/continuous-integration.

Application Packaging

The packaging of the application sits smack bang in the middle of builds and deployments and will commonly be handled by either the build tool or the deployment tool. Packaging is concerned with putting together the files needed to run the software in an appropriate format to be released.

Automated Deployments

Gone are the days of manually copying files onto servers to release software. Deployment automation ensures deployments are reliable and repeatable. This is part of the process of continuous delivery, which is a natural extension of continuous integration and is also strongly linked to DevOps.

Read more about continuous delivery here continuousdelivery.com.

Infrastructure as Code

Yet another logical progression of "automate all the things", infrastructure as code means making the configuration of bare-metal servers, virtual machines, and containers automatic. The configuration files can be stored in source control and new machines can be quickly created with identical configuration.
Without infrastructure as code, no matter how disciplined your process is your configurations will deviate from each other over time.

Application Performance Management (APM)

APM concerns the performance of your application and includes detecting bottle-necks in your application, services, and databases. This covers information on load volumes, response times, computational resources, and business transaction profiling. The goal of APM is to improve your end user experience, but this may involve detailed instrumentation right down to the code level. Your first foray into APM may simply involve detecting slow running database queries, but your end goal should be to optimise end user journeys.

Incident Management

As Matthew Syed describes eloquently in Black Box Thinking: The Surprising Truth About Success, there are two distinct modes of failure handling. These modes are illustrated with examples from aviation and healthcare.

The aviation industry converts failures and near-misses into learning. The industry accepts that there is a wider system at play that is highly complex, and that when a crisis descends there are psychological factors that impact decision making. Conversely, the medical industry has fallen into the habit of spinning failure. When something goes wrong, it is "one of those things"; an unavoidable tragedy. The fear of blame and litigation means that everyone convinces each other, and themselves, that nothing could have been done differently.

The result of these two contrasting cultures in respect of failure is that the aviation industry learns from every failure and becomes safer, whereas the medical profession fails to learn from its mistakes (although there have recently been several experiments in promoting a more aviation-style approach within the medical profession, which have been successful).

If you want to make something out of your career in web operations, you'll need to embrace every opportunity to learn from failure. It will be tempting to declare the incident someone's fault – but blame leads to defensive behaviour and will cost you the chance of preventing a similar incident later. In fact, you'll need to go further than simply avoiding blame, after you have heroically saved the day and found the root cause of a fault you will have to reign-in your bragging rights and protect those who may have cost you a lunch break. This will help to build the trust necessary to make learning possible.

Incident Response Process

So, your first job is to write a simple incident response process with a checklist you can use to guarantee your response is calm, disciplined, professional, and consistent. The process should briefly describe what constitutes an "incident", how people in the organisation can raise an incident, and the workflow for resolving an incident.

I find it valuable to add a section to the incident checklist that reiterates that "no remedial action should be taken until the root cause is known" – and that "any actions taken, whether they fix the issue or not, are carefully noted during the investigation so they can be reversed, or repeated". The incident checklist should contain the following information:

1. **Incident Manager**: a blank space for the name of the person leading the investigation into the current incident. This person must be protected from distractions (especially status updates) and be given time and space to find the problem and propose a fix. They are responsible for adding further incident managers if they need to pair up on a problem or need specialist help.

2. **Communications Manager**: a blank space for the name of the person who will handle all communications. They will act as point of contact for the stakeholders and defend the Incident Manager from the inevitable interruptions and status update requests.

3. **Stakeholders**: a pre-completed list of people who should be kept updated with information about the incident. You may have separate lists depending on the application affected, or the severity of the incident.

4. **Communication Strategy**: a checklist that reminds the communication manager about how often to issue updates to the stakeholders. The frequency may change based on the faulting application or on the severity of the incident.

5. **Escalation Strategy**: if the incident is not resolved within a certain timescale, there should be time-based escalation points to ensure the incident manager doesn't lose track of time in the heat of the investigation.

6. **Post-Incident Retrospective**: there should be space to track the post-fix investigation and the proposed actions for ensuring a similar incident doesn't happen in the future.

The importance of funnelling communications through the communications manager during an incident cannot be overstated in your incident response process. Be crystal clear on this point, and get agreement to the process from all the stakeholders before an incident occurs.

If stakeholders find out about an incident from the appointed communications manager, they will immediately feel more assured than if they find out through some other channel. In my case, because my team demonstrated such discipline during a crisis we found that the stakeholders simply thanked the communications manager for letting them know, and then calmly waited for updates. Before the incident management process was introduced, it was common for stakeholders to hover behind the person handling the incident. Needless to say, this did not help!

After each incident, the checklist can be carefully sanitised and logged for future reference on a day log, or wiki, or a similar collaboration tool. Remember to avoid using the process or checklist for blame. Keep things safe and use the trust you build to reduce the number of incidents you are required to handle, rather than exacting "incident revenge" and then having to deal with continual problems of the same kind.

Be prepared to update the incident checklist if you learn that it could be improved.

Post-incident actions should be decided collaboratively with anyone who could help to prevent a recurrence. An incident is also a wonderful opportunity to review your monitoring and alerting to see if you could have discovered the incident any earlier. This is especially the case if you found out about the incident from a customer. What could you monitor that might tell you a similar problem has occurred? There is more on this a little later in the book.

Practical Investigation Tips

When something goes wrong, it may be due to some internal trigger such as a software release or configuration change, or it may be caused by an external factor such as increased load, or an attack. You will need to eliminate internal triggers swiftly, which is why a strong audit trail is needed for releases and for configuration changes.

You'll also benefit from some techniques borrowed from philosophy and critical thinking. You don't need to study these subjects extensively to find plenty of useful information about correlation and causation. In the context of incident management, there is a simple set of causation principles:

1. Find correlations
2. Arrange everything in the correct order
3. Form a falsifiable hypothesis
4. Test the hypothesis

Dashboards are one of the keys to finding correlations. Although you may be looking at slow response times, you'll see other metrics that show changes earlier than the response time metric.

To find the root cause you will need to eliminate metrics by ordering the changes chronologically, and removing noise caused by unrelated changes. The earliest metric left in your set is a likely candidate that will lead you to the root cause.

Once you have found a smoking gun, you can form a hypothesis about what will resolve the problem and test it out. Be prepared to drop your "dead certainty" if the evidence doesn't support it. Your hypothesis should be easily falsifiable if you make a change and it doesn't resolve the problem. You can test the hypothesis on a single server to get this answer. Keep detailed notes about anything you change during your investigation.

Summary

Incident management is not about fancy tools. It is about culture, and about keeping cool under trying conditions. This makes it much harder to master than your monitoring platform, because psychology is harder than charts; but the payoff from a good incident management process that is executed with the right mindset is gargantuan compared to using just monitoring platforms without the necessary human elements.

Metric Collection

When it comes to metric collection, people can get a bit hung up on the observer effect. Some people are reluctant to install an agent on a server. There is no method of collecting data that won't consume some of the resource you intend to measure.

This shouldn't put you off collecting data, not only is the agent lightweight in terms of resource use, it is also one of the most valuable ways to use those resources.

The Datadog agent typically uses <1% CPU, 50MB RAM, <50KB/minute of network - help.datadoghq.com/hc/en-us/articles/203034929.

The Datadog agent takes a snapshot of your selected metrics every 15 seconds or so, and queues it for onward transmission to the cloud monitoring platform. It also exposes a simple API for your application to send custom metrics for onward transmission. Only simple collection, filtering, and forwarding is performed by the agent. All the serious data crunching occurs in the cloud once the data has been received by the platform.

If you don't already have a monitoring platform, you can set up a free account on Datadog and follow along with the examples in this book. You can sign up at:

Datadog www.datadoghq.com

The free trial of Datadog runs for 14 days with all the standard features, including dashboards, monitoring, and alerting. Datadog also have a free community edition for up to five servers, which lets you experiment with dashboards, but without monitoring and alerting.

Once you have signed up, you'll be able to follow all the practical examples in the next few chapters.

Agent Architecture

The diagram on the following page shows the Datadog agent architecture, with metrics arriving from the collector and custom metrics API and being sent to the monitoring platform by the forwarder. Most metric collection agents will follow a similar architecture.

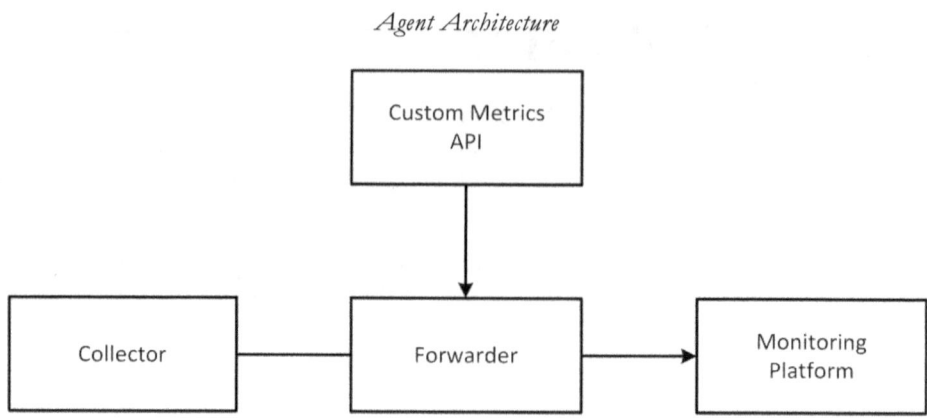

Agent Architecture

Custom Metrics

The custom metrics API allows you to forward technical metrics such as queue sizes, but you can also use it to send business-related metrics like number of forms submitted, or the number of checkouts started and completed.

Some organisations use these business metrics following a release to ensure that the latest features and changes are not negatively impacting key business goals. For example, one holiday booking service monitors many business metrics such as the number of bookings, and the value of bookings. If a release negatively impacts these business metrics, they will roll it back.

You can also use these business metrics for monitoring and alerting. If the number of bookings or the value of bookings drops below a threshold, or falls by a certain amount, you can raise an alarm to have the unusual system behaviour investigated even though there may be no apparent technical fault.

Agent Configuration

The Datadog agent can be installed on your host using a single command. You can grab the command from your account in the **Integrations -> Agent** area of the Datadog poral. The command is ready to run, and includes your API key, which you should keep secret.

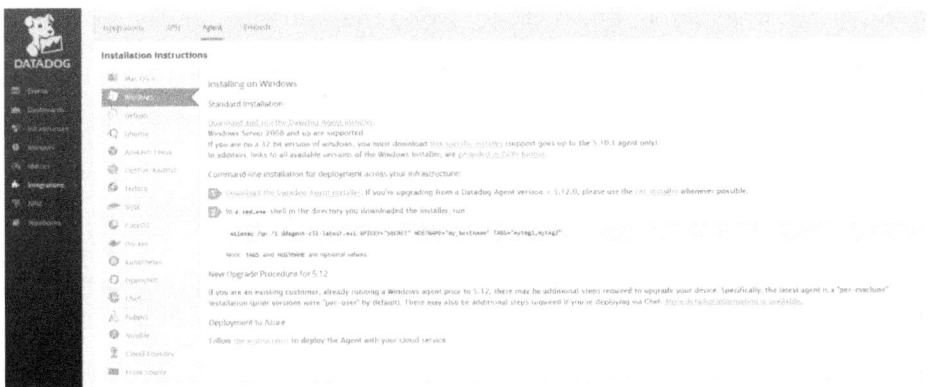

```
msiexec /qn /i ddagent-cli-latest.msi APIKEY="SECRET"
HOSTNAME="my_hostname" TAGS="mytag1,mytag2"
```

Once you run this command on a server, the Datadog agent and its associated configuration will be installed. The agent will immediately start collecting some basic metrics, but you can add additional integrations to collect more data.

The full list of integrations (sometimes referred to as "apps") in the Datadog portal under **Integrations -> Integrations**.

Settings

Datadog installs with a good set of default settings. These can be found by opening the Agent Manager UI on Windows, or by opening the location /etc/dd-agent/datadog.conf on a Linux machine. A simplified configuration for Datadog is shown below. It contains the address of the Datadog API, your secret key, a set of tags that you can use to filter the data later.

```
[Main]

dd_url: https://app.datadoghq.com
api_key: YOUR-API-KEY
tags: role:example,location:london

gce_updated_hostname: yes

log_to_event_viewer: no
```

Tags are important when you come to break down groups of hosts for dashboards, monitoring, and alerting. Using the colon-syntax gives titles to use in your tagging; so instead of using plain tags such as "webfarm", "database", and "eventqueue", you should prefix each tag with "role:", like this:

- role:webfarm
- role:database
- role:eventqueue

When you come to filter your hosts later, you can type "role" and Datadog will suggest different roles. You can use multiple tags to add servers to many different groups depending on your server architecture.

I have found the following tags useful:

- Tag how the host is used with "role:", for example "crm", "database", "messagebus"

- Tag the datacentre with "location:", such as "london", "newyork", "euro-dr"

The configuration for each integration is also stored in text files on the system. Integrations can be enabled on Windows using the "Enable" option in the Agent Manager UI, or on other systems by renaming the YAML files. Here are some examples of integrations for two common integrations.

Win32 Event Log

This sample event log configuration demonstrates how you can collect all error and critical event logs from both the system and application event logs.

```
init_config:

instances:
    -   tags:
            - myTag
        type:
            - Error
            - Critical
        log_file:
            - System
            - Application
```

```
        message_filters:
            - '-%The Open Procedure for service "BITS" in
DLL "C:\Windows\System32\bitsperf.dll" failed%'
    -    tags:
            - myTag
        type:
            - Information
        log_file:
            - System
            - Application
        message_filters:
            - '%collector was unresponsive for too long.
Restarting...%'
```

You can use message filters to include or exclude event logs. The filter is a string to match to the event, using the percent sign (%) as a wildcard. When you use an include filter, only matching events will be forwarded. If you start a filter with a minus sign (-) it will exclude matches. Watch out for the slightly confusing minus-sign issue; each line in your config file starts with a minus sign. To write an exclude filter, the minus sign must be inside the quotes.

```
- '%Include Filter%'
- '-%Exclude Filter%'
```

The config example removes the common BITS event log entries, and adds events that match the collector unresponsive error that will warn you that an agent isn't running normally.

IIS

The IIS configuration can be very simple. This simply monitors the local IIS instance and attaches a tag for filtering in the monitoring portal.
init_config:

```
instances:
    -    host: .
        tags:
            - myTag
```

Hopefully these example configuration files give you an idea about how easy it is to set up integrations. The agent is installed with a set of example files that are usable in common scenarios.

Adding More Integrations

To collect more data from your host you can review the list of integration on the Datadog portal. There is a comprehensive set of instructions for each integration that you can follow when you need to. Head to **Integrations -> Integrations**, select the one you are interested in, and follow the instructions in the Configuration tab.

Integration Configuration Instructions

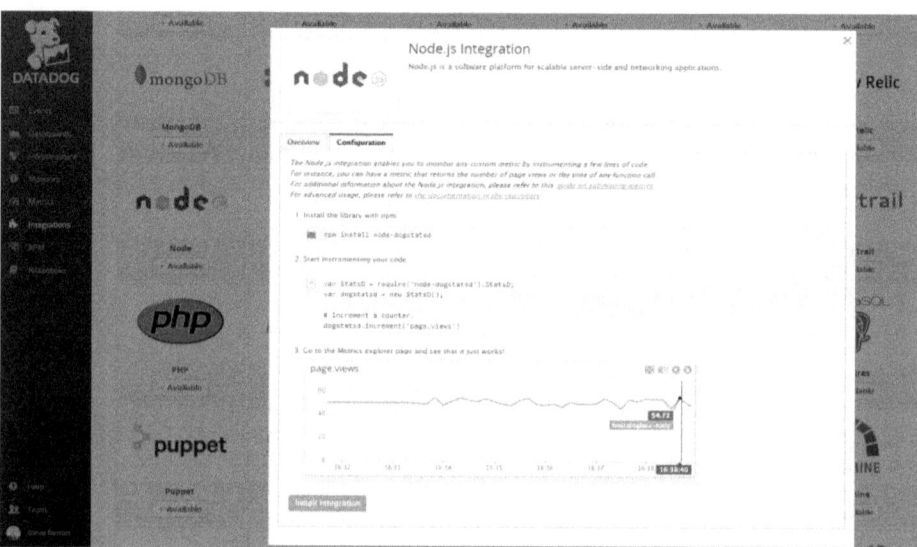

Because the Datadog agent is configured with simple text files, you can treat your configuration as code and use your DevOps toolchain to author, release, and configure Datadog on each server.

Shortly after setting up an agent or add an integration, you will start seeing event logs and metrics on the monitoring platform. If you have added an integration and can't see the numbers, make sure you enabled the integration on the server. You can see the enabled integrations for each machine by selecting the "Infrastructure" menu and choosing a server.

Apps Running (click to see app metrics)

iis ntp system

If you don't see data, check the agent status to ensure your configuration is valid.

See this article for more on agent status and information help.datadoghq.com/hc/en-us/articles/203764635.

Summary

Most metric collection follows the agent pattern, especially where the monitoring platform is hosted in the cloud. The agent is so lightweight, it shouldn't cause resource contention. You can collect a wide range of metrics, which can be configured with simple text files. You can also send custom metrics, which allows you to track the data that really matters to your application.

You should apply the same process to the release and configuration of your agents as you do to your own software. Manually deploying, configuring, and updating agents is not a scalable solution.

Event Log Aggregation

Depending on your application architecture, you may be logging events to one of many places. If you are working on many applications, perhaps you are logging to several places on a server. Add multiple servers into the mix, and the information you need to obtain when an application error occurs can be spread all over the place.

A monitoring platform allows you to collect the system logs, security logs, application logs, and any other logs into a single place where you can see them all in one view, group them into similar errors, search them, and (ultimately) fix them.

The simplest way to do this is to ensure that your application logs to the system event log, then simply forward all event logs to your monitoring platform.

Event Log Aggregation

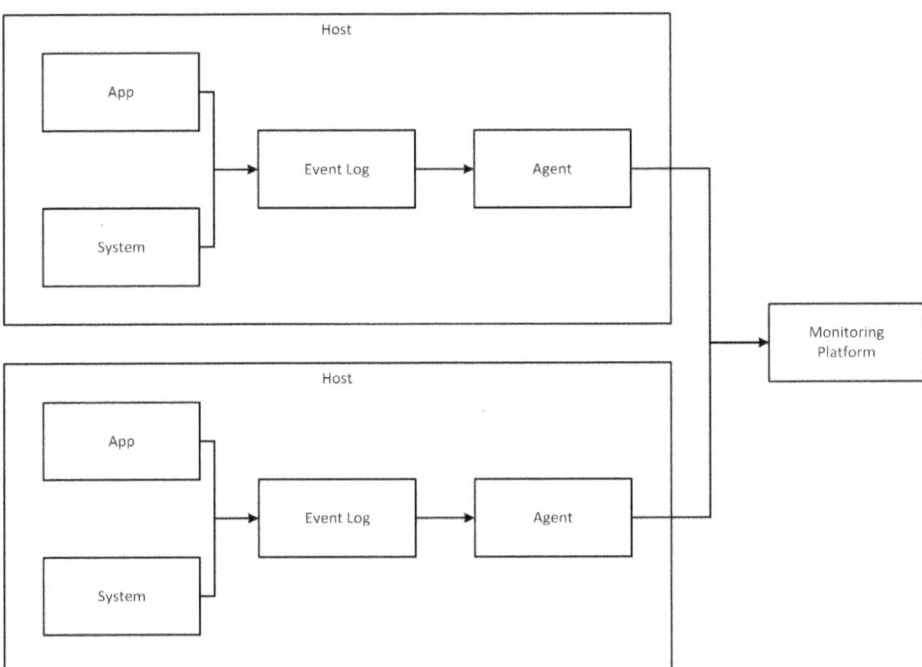

Aggregating your event logs reduces the amount of time people need to spend connected to individual servers. Aggregated event logs also reveal an otherwise hidden problem: you have a lot of errors in your event logs and nobody is reading them. Making a problem visible is the first step towards solving it, but you may find the number of errors overwhelming.

Fear not, because there is a simple way to break the problem down.

The Three Fs

If you haven't been reviewing your event logs, aggregating them all will cause a deluge of information. Much of this will be noise and until you deal with it, you won't spot critical error logs. You may feel that you are now worse off, but the only difference to how you were handling things before is that you now know the size of the problem.

It will be impossible to sift through every error on day one, but you don't have to; all you need is the event log processing priority technique known as The Three Fs. Just pick the most frequently occurring event in your combined log and decide which of these three actions to take:

- **Finesse**: arrange for better quality information to be included in the log entry

- **Fix**: fix the underlying problem

- **Filter**: de-classify the log entry so it isn't forwarded to the monitoring platform

Here is a quick example for each "F".

Your application may raise an error that looks problematic, but there isn't enough information about the data involved in the error to reproduce the problem. The error should be finessed by adding additional information when the application logs the error.

Another error may tell you that your application raised an "Object reference not set to an instance of an object", and you can see there is a missing null-check on the line identified in the error. The error should be fixed by adding the null check.

Some operating systems like to tell you every few minutes that "The BITS service failed to initialize". A quick investigation will confirm that this is normal behaviour, and you can filter that event out by updating your agent configuration.

Until you get your errors under control, your simple task is to repeat the Finesse-Fix-Filter process, targeting the next most common error each time.

The ideal outcome of your work will be an event timeline that looks like the figure below.

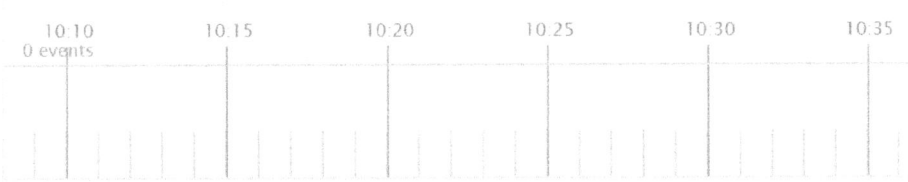

0 matching events in the past hour

This is the kind of timeline that will help you spot a problem before your customers do. In fact, this isn't just about handling incidents, this kind of timeline will also catch bugs that would otherwise be undetectable. Customers run far more scenarios than you will during your testing. These scenarios are often much more realistic, what with them being real customers using your real production system.

Asymptote: Don't Despair

Don't despair if you don't get to zero errors, the goal of zero errors is an asymptote; you will get closer and closer to zero, but going an entire week with no errors being logged is highly unlikely.

The figure below shows a typical event timeline after a substantial and prolonged attempt to achieve the dream. This figure shows aggregated events across nearly fifty servers in two geographical locations, running applications, services, databases, load balancers, caches, and integrations.

Typical Event Timeline

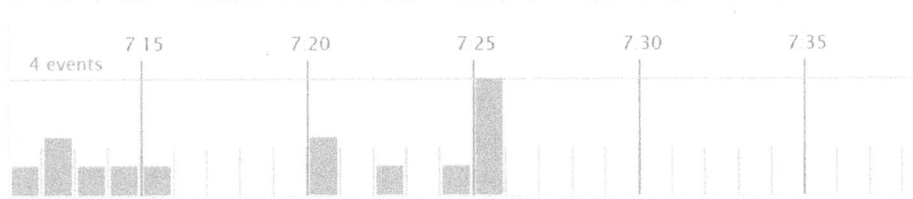

24 matching events from Aug 17, 7:11AM - Aug 17, 8:11AM

You can judge the success of your event-reducing campaign using the following sentence:

When a fault appears in the event log that requires
action, it is spotted and action is taken.

This is the purpose of all that hard work – to make it possible to see fault signals that would otherwise be lost in the noise of too many events.

Zipped Events

Your monitoring platform will probably zip up your events, so even when there are many errors in the selected period, multiple instances of the same event will be zipped into a single event description below the timeline.

This means you may only be looking at four errors, even though there are forty individual entries.

Zipped events are usually followed by an indication of the number of occurrences they represent, much like the figure below, which shows a single event log entry that represents 7 events in a timeline, represented visually with red squares and with a note of the count:

Zipped Events

Inner Exception:
Exception type: IOException
The process cannot access the file because it is being used by another process.
at System.IO.__Error.WinIOError(Int32 errorCode, String maybeFullPath)
at System.IO.FileStream.Init(String path, FileMode mode, FileAccess access, Int32 options, SECURITY_ATTRIBUTES secAttrs, String msgPath, Boolean bFromProxy, B
at System.IO.FileStream..ctor(String path, FileMode mode, FileAccess access, File'
Show more
Updated 3 hours ago · Created 9 hours ago · Add comment · Lower priority

7 events ▪ ▪ ▪ ▪ ▪ ▪

This may help both in terms of reducing the noise created by an outage that temporarily generates lots of the same error (for example a brief network interruption), and in determining common errors that should be targeted by the three Fs.

Information Radiator

If you have a wallboard available to display information, the event timeline is a good view to stick on there. It may not be the choice of film directors, who would much rather show one of your dashboards stuffed with charts (coming up in the chapter on Dashboards); but seeing events streaming in real time will help you be first to react when things go wrong.

As with most of the information you will be displaying for the purposes of web operations, beware of who it is visible to. Exception information can contain sensitive data, so you'll want to ensure you have thought about the security of the information being displayed. Don't stick your wallboard in reception!

And one final word of caution. When the event information is in front of you all the time, your brain will learn to filter out errors that are not important. Don't let this be the role of your brain – apply the three Fs with rigor and empty out your event timeline to make all errors worth reading.

Summary

You need to aggregate your event logs because until you do, you don't know the size of your logging problem. You can use the three Fs to reduce the number of event logs in your view, aiming for the asymptote of zero errors.

Once you have your errors under control, each item that appears will provide you with powerful information about the health of your applications, services, and infrastructure.

Dashboards

You will need dashboards in two distinct situations. There are "everyday" dashboards that you will view all the time that will tell you at a glance if everything is healthy or not, and there are "detailed" dashboards that you will use to investigate a problem.

Your everyday dashboards should be trimmed to just the fundamental information that tells you if everything is okay. Ideally you could still tell whether things are working well even if you took off your glasses, or stood across the room. These dashboards have one job; to catch your attention when there is a problem. If someone passes your desk and says "Hey, is everything alright?", your instinctive reaction should be to look at your everyday dashboard (or dashboards).

Ideally, you would have a wallboard for each everyday dashboard. You can cycle through them all on a single wallboard, but the effect of flicking through pages is that people don't notice changes as fast. This isn't just because of the delay in getting to the dashboard that is trying to speak to you, it is also because if the screen is changing routinely, you won't notice that corner-of-the-eye movement that may signal the start of an incident.

Your detailed dashboards are on standby for when you need to drill down to investigate a problem. You don't want these dashboards up on the wall, you just want to use them on demand during an incident, and afterwards when you try to piece together a timeline of what happened.

So, your monitoring platform is going to be full of dashboards. There will be dashboards automatically generated for specific integrations you have, such as SQL server, HAProxy, and IIS. There will also be standard dashboards for network throughput, disk I/O, and for each server sending data. Despite this, your everyday dashboard will almost certainly be a custom dashboard.

Custom Dashboards

Things have just got serious. This is, in fact, exactly the information I wanted when I first started looking at web operations. What do you add to your first custom dashboard? Browsing through the metrics made available just by collecting data from servers is overwhelming. Just look at the scrollbar that lists the different information that you can plot; it is hard to pick just a few key numbers for your everyday custom dashboard.

Metrics Explorer

Graph:

```
|
iis.httpd_request_method.delete
iis.httpd_request_method.get
iis.httpd_request_method.head
iis.httpd_request_method.options
iis.httpd_request_method.post
iis.httpd_request_method.put
iis.httpd_request_method.trace
iis.net.bytes_rcvd
iis.net.bytes_sent
iis.net.bytes.total
```

Fear not. Create an empty dashboard and add the following foundation metrics that are a good broad brush for many scenarios.

The following four charts apply to pretty much all servers:

CPU: The minimum idle percentage per host. If one of the lines hits the bottom of the chart and stays there, we may have a problem.

Memory: The minimum usable percentage per host. If one of the lines hits the bottom of the chart and stays there, we may have a problem.

I/O: The max reads per host in kb/s and the max writes per host in kb/s (inverted so writes hang below the zero line). We can watch for unusual behaviour, such as rapid spikes in I/O. This is especially useful as an early indicator for other problems, for example a database is being inappropriately hammered, as high I/O against a database suggests something is reading out entire tables, which is almost always an accident.

- **Network**: max inbound kb/s per host and outbound kb/s per host (inverted so outbound hangs below the zero line).
- The following four charts apply to pretty much all web servers:

- **Connections**: The max number of connections per host. Sudden spikes in connections indicate bad robots, or even attacks (including unwitting attacks).

- **Bytes**: The max bytes in per host and the max bytes out per host (inverted so bytes out hang below the zero line).

- **Requests**: The sum of requests per second across all hosts for each HTTP verb.

- **Errors**: The sum of HTTP not found errors across all hosts.

Here is the custom board. It isn't perfect, but it is a start.

Custom Dashboard

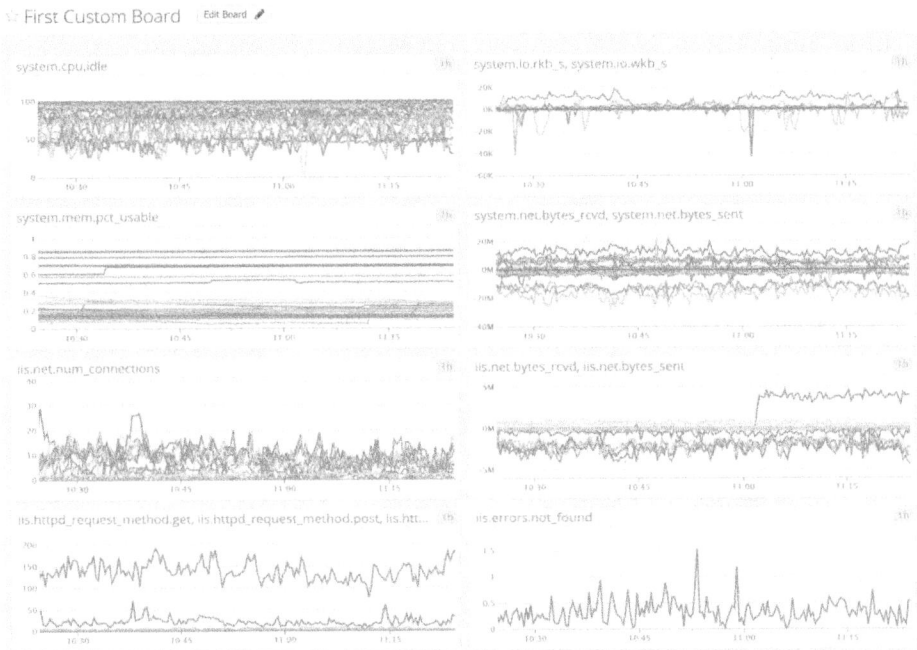

If you are using a different monitoring platform, you should be able to achieve the same results. The JSON configuration contains the two main items you will need to translate, a query "q" and the chart type "type". Where the number has been inverted, for example bytes out, or IIS bytes sent, you can see the query is multiplied by -1.

Datadog, and many other tools have different kinds of dashboard. A wallboard allows you to specify the time series for each individual chart, whereas a time-board allows you to control all charts from a single time series control. The time-board allows you to quickly update all charts on the board to show different resolutions of data, which can reveal longer term trends.

Metric Queries

Datadog will write queries for you based on what you select when adding a chart in the visual tools, but you can also write your own queries too.

Read more on queries here help.datadoghq.com/hc/en-us/articles/204820019.

The structure of a query is as follows:

- **Function** (min, max, sum, avg, etc)

- **Metric** (system.cpu.idle, system.mem.pct_usable. etc)

- **Scope** (tags to filter hosts to include in the query)

- **Grouping** (host, device, etc)

- **Expression** (for example: * 10)

The next section contains examples with the queries broken into chunks, and the resulting chart shown below.

Average CPU

```
Function: avg
Metric: system.cpu.idle
Scope: {*}

Query: avg:system.cpu.idle{*}
```

The Average Idle CPU for All Hosts

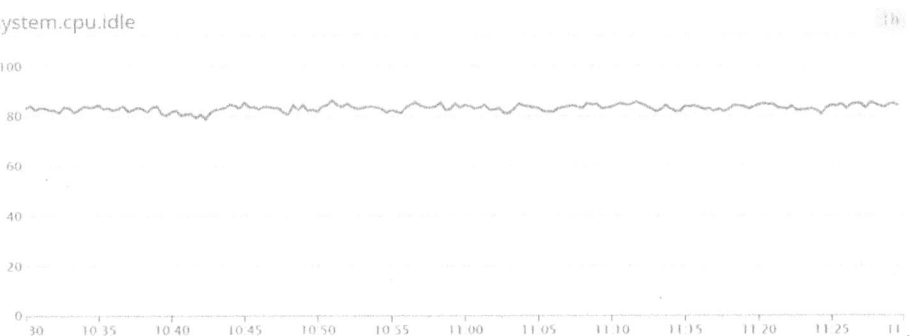

Minimum CPU

```
Function: min
Metric: system.cpu.idle
Scope: {*}

Query: min:system.cpu.idle{*}
```

The Minimum Idle CPU for All Hosts

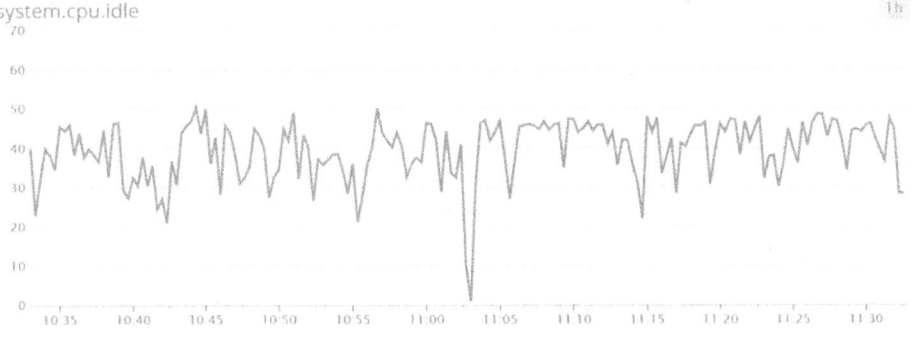

Group by Host

```
Function: min
Metric: system.cpu.idle
Scope: {*}
Group: by {host}
```

```
Query: min:system.cpu.idle{*} by {host}
```

Minimum CPU Grouped by Host

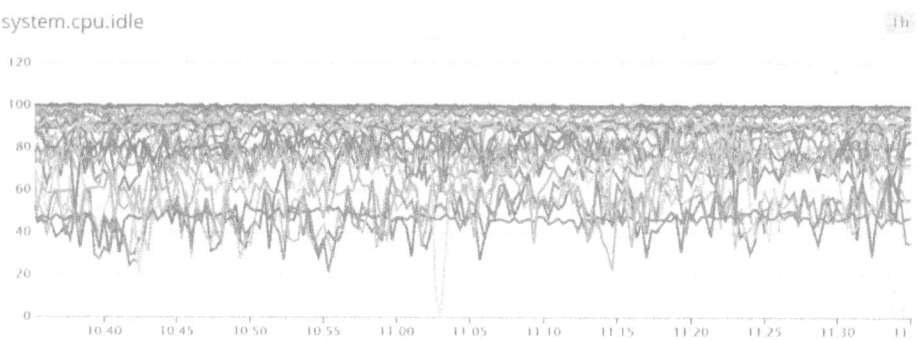

Limiting Scope

```
Function: min
Metric: system.cpu.idle
Scope: {role:farm}
Group: by {host}

Query: min:system.cpu.idle{role:farm} by {host}
```

Minimum CPU Limited to "farm role"

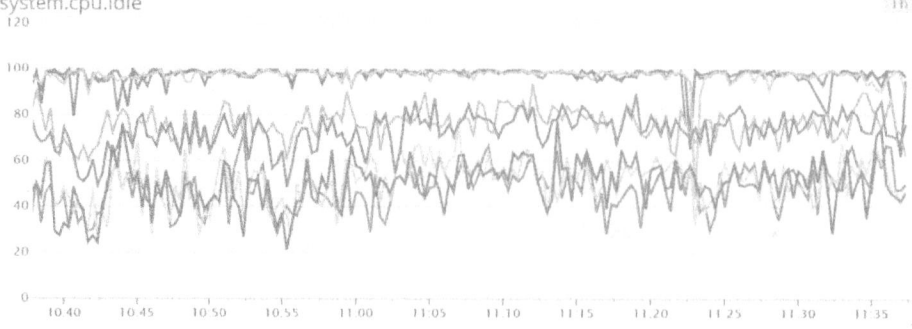

Modifying Values with Expressions

```
Function: min
Metric: system.cpu.idle
Scope: {role:farm}
Group: by {host}
Expression: * 0.5

Query: min:system.cpu.idle{role:farm} by {host} * 0.5
```

Minimum CPU Divided by Two

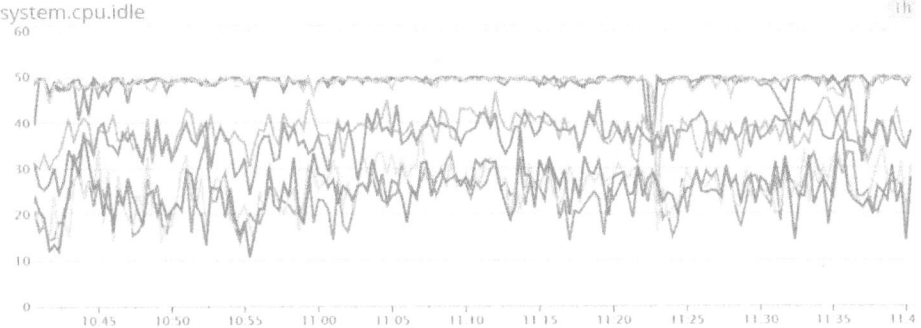

JSON Chart Samples

Although you can edit these charts manually, you can also configure the raw JSON representation. Some sample configurations are shown below.

CPU

The metric for idle CPU is system.cpu.idle. This is the amount of CPU not currently in use by the system or by a user. The configuration below plots the idle CPU on a line chart. You can see the query near the top, with the key: "q".

```
{
  "requests": [
    {
```

```
      "q": "min:system.cpu.idle{*} by {host}",
      "type": "line",
      "conditional_formats": [],
      "aggregator": "avg"
    }
  ],
  "viz": "timeseries",
  "autoscale": true
}
```

Memory

The percentage of available memory is stored in the
system.mem.pct_usable metric. The configuration that follows
queries the minimum system.mem.pct_usable for each host, and
plots it on a line chart.

```
{
  "requests": [
    {
      "q": "min:system.mem.pct_usable{*} by {host}",
      "type": "line",
      "conditional_formats": [],
      "aggregator": "avg"
    }
  ],
  "viz": "timeseries",
  "autoscale": true
}
```

I/O

The I/O information is found in the reads and writes in kilobytes per
second. The metrics are named system.io.rkb_s and system.io.wkb_s
respectively.

The configuration that follows selects the maximum system.io.rkb_s for each host, and the maximum system.io.wkb_s for each host and plots it on a line chart.

The writes have been multiplied by minus one to show them on the opposite side of the zero-line on the chart. This allows you to easily see the read trends vs the write trends.

```
{
  "requests": [
    {
      "q": "max:system.io.rkb_s{*} by {host}",
      "type": "line",
      "conditional_formats": [],
      "aggregator": "avg"
    },
    {
      "q": "max:system.io.wkb_s{*} by {host} * - 1",
      "type": "line"
    }
  ],
  "viz": "timeseries",
  "autoscale": true
}
```

Network

The network bytes metrics are divided between inbound and outbound bytes. You'll find the numbers in system.net.bytes_rcvd and system.net.bytes_sent respectively.

The configuration below selects the maximum values for each host and plots it on a line chart. Once again, the trick of investing one of the metrics allows you to easily see the inbound group vs the outbound group.

```
{
  "requests": [
    {
      "q": "max:system.net.bytes_rcvd{*} by {host}",
      "type": "line",
      "conditional_formats": [],
      "aggregator": "avg"
```

```
    },
    {
        "q": "max:system.net.bytes_sent{*} by {host} * -
1",
        "type": "line"
    }
  ],
  "viz": "timeseries",
  "autoscale": true
}
```

IIS Connections

The number of concurrent IIS connections is stored in the metric:
iis.net.num_connections.

Below is the configuration that selects the maximum number of
connections for each host and shows the data on a line chart.

```
{
  "requests": [
    {
        "q": "max:iis.net.num_connections{*} by {host}",
        "type": "line",
        "conditional_formats": [],
        "aggregator": "avg"
    }
  ],
  "viz": "timeseries",
  "autoscale": true
}
```

IIS Bytes

The metric for IIS bytes allows you to see both the inbound volume
(iis.net.bytes_rcvd) and the outbound volume (iis.net.bytes_sent).
The configuration below selects the maximum inbound, and the maximum
outbound bytes. The familiar inversion trick has been applied to outbound
bytes.

```
{
  "requests": [
    {
      "q": "max:iis.net.bytes_rcvd{*} by {host}",
      "type": "line",
      "conditional_formats": [],
      "aggregator": "avg"
    },
    {
      "q": "avg:iis.net.bytes_sent{*} by {host} * - 1",
      "type": "line"
    }
  ],
  "viz": "timeseries",
  "autoscale": true
}
```

IIS Requests

A single IIS connection may have multiple IIS requests. These are available in metrics grouped by the request verb, for example GET, POST, PUT, and DELETE.

The configuration below obtains the number of requests for all HTTP verbs across all hosts (not per host), and displays them on a line chart.

```
{
  "requests": [
    {
      "q": "sum:iis.httpd_request_method.get{*}",
      "type": "line",
      "conditional_formats": [],
      "aggregator": "avg"
    },
    {
      "q": "sum:iis.httpd_request_method.post{*}",
      "type": "line"
    },
    {
      "q": "sum:iis.httpd_request_method.put{*}",
```

```
        "type": "line"
      },
      {
        "q": "sum:iis.httpd_request_method.head{*}",
        "type": "line"
      },
      {
        "q": "sum:iis.httpd_request_method.trace{*}",
        "type": "line"
      },
      {
        "q": "sum:iis.httpd_request_method.trace{*}",
        "type": "line"
      },
      {
        "q": "sum:iis.httpd_request_method.delete{*}",
        "type": "line"
      },
      {
        "q": "sum:iis.httpd_request_method.options{*}",
        "type": "line"
      }
    ],
    "viz": "timeseries",
    "autoscale": true
}
```

IIS Errors

There is a separate metric named iis.errors.not_found that contains the count of HTTP 404 errors.

The following configuration obtains this value across all hosts and displays it on a line chart.

```
{
  "requests": [
    {
      "q": "sum:iis.errors.not_found{*}",
      "type": "line",
      "conditional_formats": [],
```

```
        "aggregator": "avg"
    }
  ],
  "viz": "timeseries",
  "autoscale": true
}
```

Learning to Spot Anomalies

Your next job is to stare at this dashboard long enough to get an instinctive feel for what is healthy in your context. Watching everything running for a few days (with breaks of course) will imprint the normal patterns on your brain. Once this happens, you'll feel that there is a problem before you even know why.

There are several things you will learn as you familiarise yourself with your custom dashboard.

- You will see changes in the charts that are not problems, for example you'll see regular spikes caused by batch operations and slumps caused by your customers going to bed.

- You will see changes that correlate with reported problems.

- You will have problems reported for which you can't see any change.

Before long, you'll get a strong feeling for what is normal and you'll be ready to make that tacit knowledge explicit.

You can improve the chances of spotting an error on your wallboards by avoiding screen cycling (the practice of showing different screens on the same board ever few seconds). Instead, you should keep the same dashboard on the same screen and add additional screens if you need to. When a dashboard is permanently displayed, changes start to become visible to your subconscious. If you keep swapping the dashboards, the on-screen changes become part of what your brain considers "normal" and you'll be slower to spot problems.

Markers

Once you understand the normal behaviour of your charts, you can add markers to help highlight problems. For example, if you are monitoring the synchronization speed of SQL replication, add a line at "ten seconds" to show that you expect the replication times to be largely below 10 seconds.

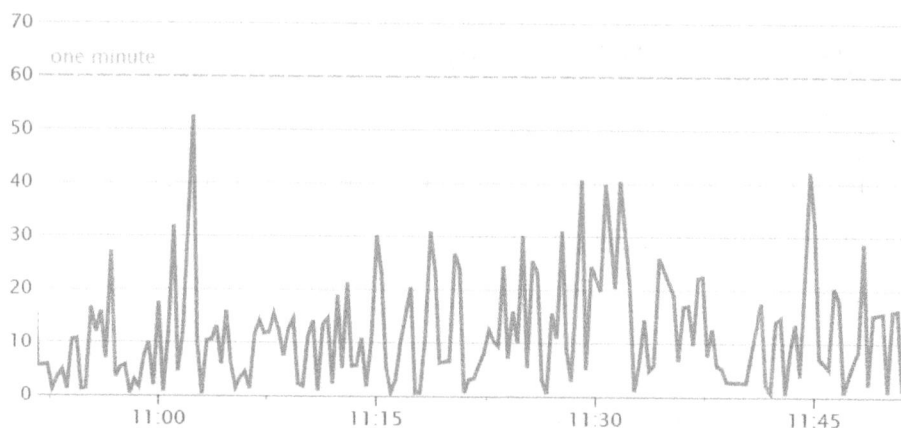

One Minute Marker

This is useful because most dashboards will size the chart to its data. If you are showing data over one hour and the replication latency has been 300 seconds for that whole period, the chart may appear normal even though you have a major problem. With the marker in place you'll see that there is a problem because when things are fine the marker line appears at the top of the chart, and when there is a problem it will race to the bottom as the data escapes the normal bounds.

Markers also tell everyone else what normal behaviour looks like, even though they haven't sat staring at the lines for as long as you. This helps to make each chart expressive.

If you expect the number to be within a range, add a lower and higher range marker to denote the expected range.

Fifty to One Hundred Range Marker

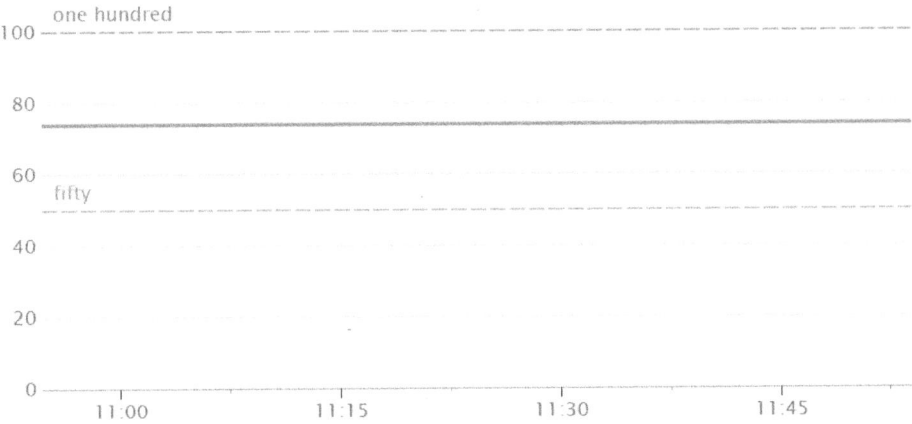

You can also use multiple markers to show warning and error values, use labels of "warning" and "error" to help any colour-blind people on your team.

Warning and Error Markers

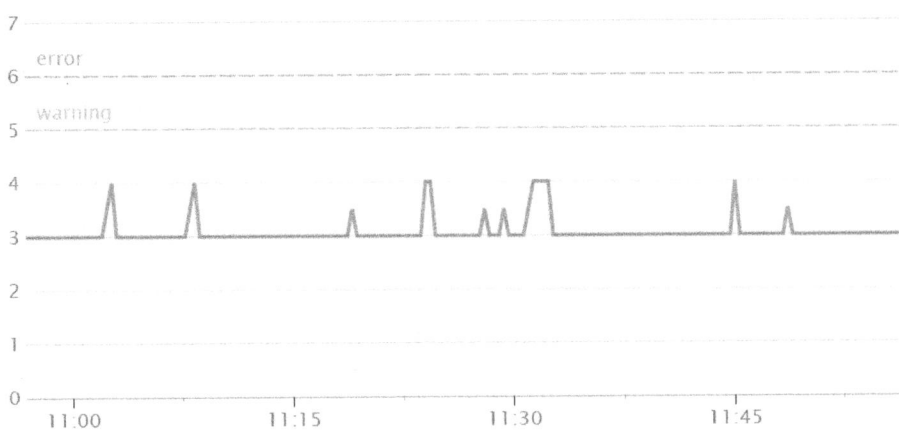

When naming markers, I always use text, for example "ten seconds", rather than numbers. This ensures your marker text doesn't cause confusion when placed close to the labels on the axis.

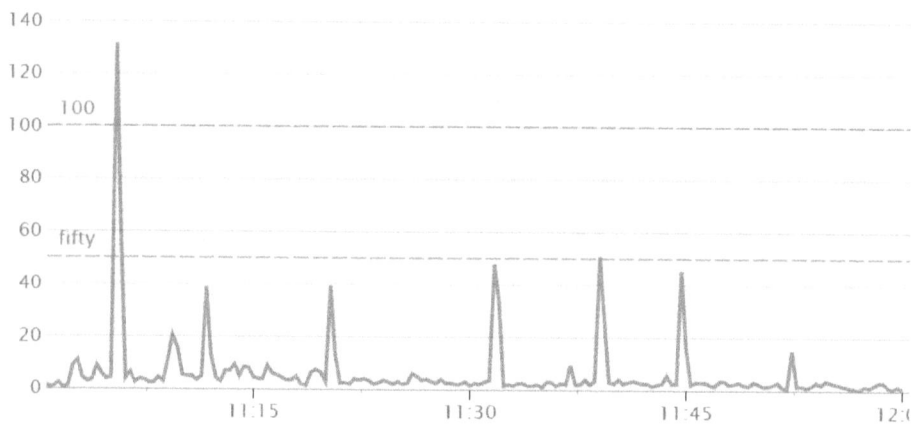

Markers make anomalies easier to see, and help to spread the knowledge about normal system behaviour.

Metrics

Each time you handle an incident, or have a near miss, you should consider updating your custom dashboard. What metrics could you add that would give you an earlier indication of a problem, and what metrics are not paying for their screen space. Keep adjusting your custom dashboard metrics to ensure you are getting plenty of strong signals and no noise.

One of the applications I worked on recently used an eventual consistency architecture with queues to store events until they could be delivered. The health of the system could be determined simply by charting the size of the queues, and the age of the oldest event in the queue. These charts, combined with markers to reveal normal sizes and ages, made problems instantly visible.

Two queues are shown below, the top one is healthy, and the one below it has a problem. These charts are visually very different, which makes it easier to spot when something has gone wrong. This is an important consideration when choosing both the metric to chart, and the kind of chart used to display it.

Healthy Chart

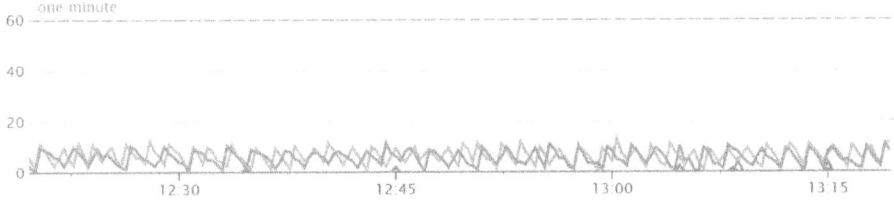

Unhealthy Chart

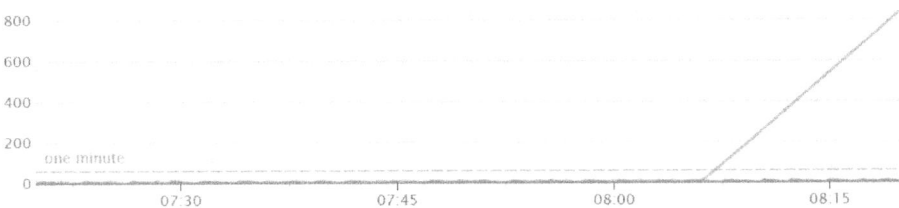

Chart Types

Another way to make your dashboards more revealing is to experiment with alternate chart types. All the example charts below display the same data using different styles. This helps to demonstrate the strengths of each type of chart in different circumstances. You may want to display the same metric in multiple charts on a dashboard to visualise different aspects of the metric.

Line Chart

Line charts are good for displaying chronological data and are particularly strong when you want to see how one line might diverge from other lines of the same kind. In the chart below, I can see that the metrics from two hosts behave in a comparable way.

Line Chart

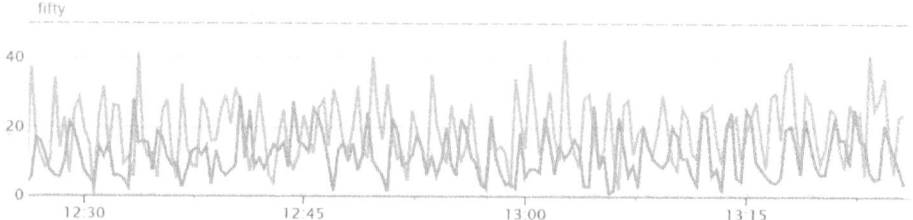

Line charts are great for determining the smoking gun when you are investigating an incident – you can look at many metrics to find "the first spike" that relates to the incident. For example, you may see several metrics going off the chart, memory, CPU, and disk – but you can work out that it was the disk I/O spike that was earliest of the warning metrics and narrow your investigation.

Area Chart

Area charts are good for visualising total utilisation across multiple hosts. If you were interested in how many requests per second you were serving across your whole web farm, the area display lets you see the total as well as the distribution between nodes in your web farm. Both the total and the distribution can indicate different problems.

Area Chart

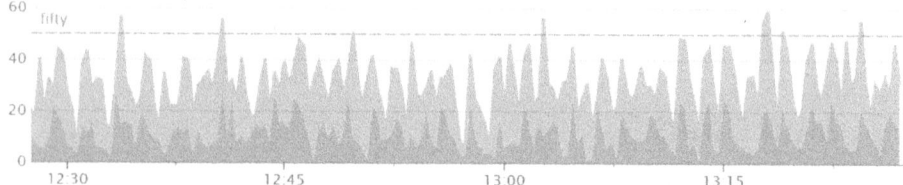

Column Chart

The column chart shows information in a similar way to the area chart, but grouped per time slice. Depending on the size of the chart, the bars will adjust to represent different time periods, but the example shows a column per minute. You can effectively zoom in and out by changing the time slice, for example to see utilisation per hour, day, month, etc.

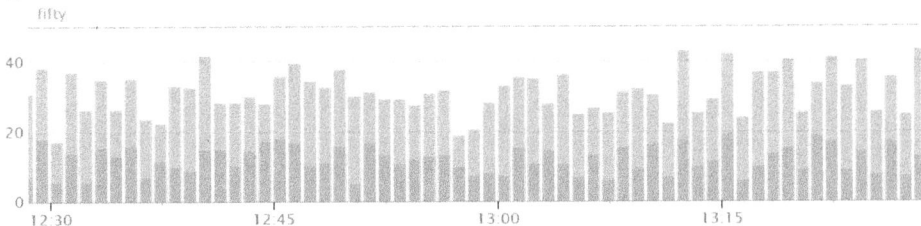

Column Chart

Heat Map

Heat maps highlighted the edges of the metric, by showing a minimum and maximum value per time slice. This allows you to quickly see outlying values at both ends of the scale easily.

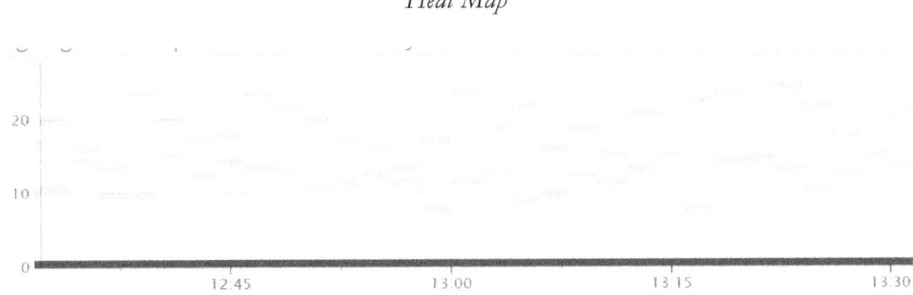

Heat Map

Distribution Chart

A distribution chart displays information from the time slice non-chronologically. Instead, it groups the data into counts per value. This allows you to see the most common values, and how far out the outliers are. In the example below, most of the data is on the left, but there are outliers shown between 10 and 11, and at 16.

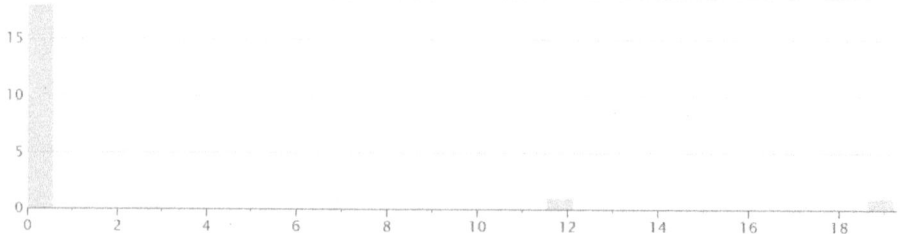

Distribution Chart

Distribution charts are useful because they don't hide small numbers of outliers like many of the other chart types may (as each plot point represents an average of data collected around that time).

Top List

A top list simply groups the metric either from highest to lowest, or vice versa. This can be useful if you want to find out which servers have the least free space on a disk, or the most requests per second. The top list is generated using the dashboard time (i.e. the past hour), but the top list is not displayed chronologically.

Top List

8e-3	d:
1e-2	l:
0.053	q:
0.079	f:
0.17	s:

Pie Chart

There is no value in a pie chart, so you won't find any in this book. Most of the information you are dealing with is chronological, which makes pie charts a terrible choice anyhow.

For more information on why you should avoid pie charts in general, visit www.stevefenton.co.uk/2009/04/pie-charts-are-bad/.

Time Indicators

The dashboard usually controls the start and end time for all the charts, which can help for event correlation. It is possible to show charts for a different start and end time; if you use this, you'll need to learn to check the selection on a per chart basis. For example, the chart may have an indicator that confirms the displayed period, for example "1h" for one hour and "1w" for one week.

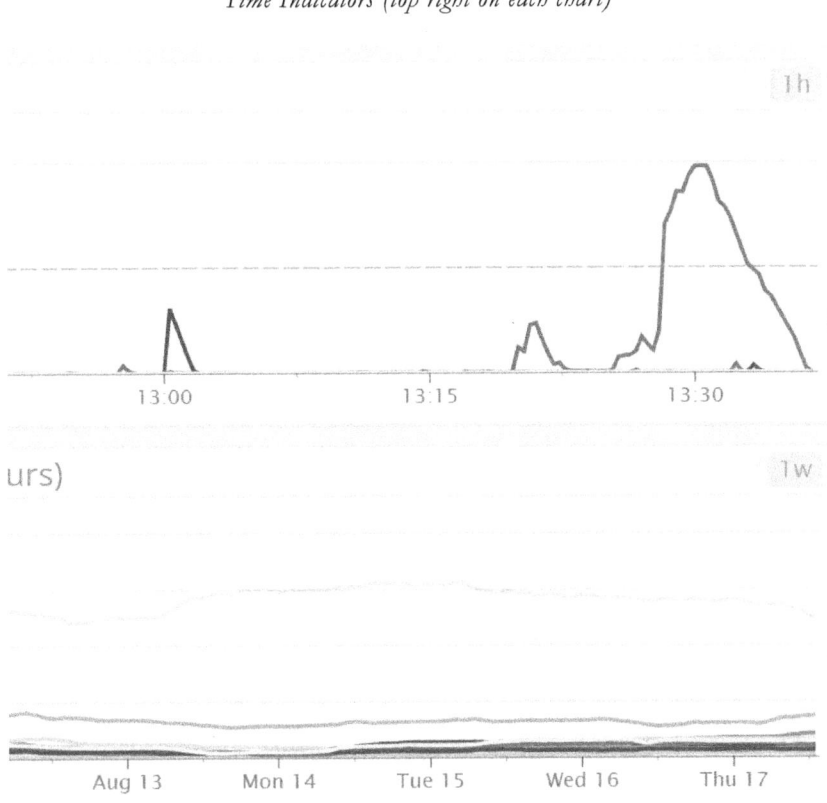

Time Indicators (top right on each chart)

When choosing the timescale of your charts, you will have to make a trade-off between resolution around the current time and visibility of trends.

If you want to detect changes in behaviour earlier, a short timescale of one hour gives you more data points for the current moment in time. This will help you to see changes sooner.

If you want to understand trends, using longer timescales make trends more apparent. The examples below show how trends become apparent when you zoom out, but remember that the resolution around what is happening right now will be lower.

- Narrower ranges amplify changes
- Wider ranges amplify trends

Here are some examples using the number of IIS connections:

One Hour Chart

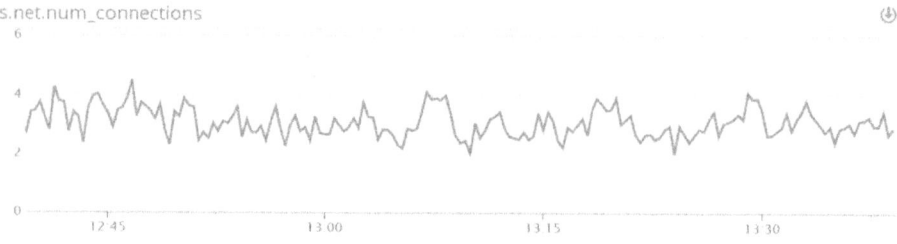

Twenty-Four Hour Chart

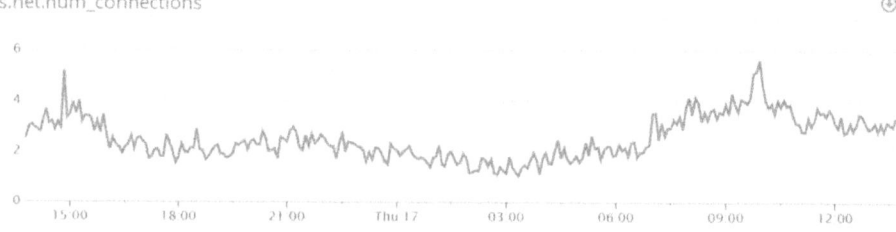

One Week Chart

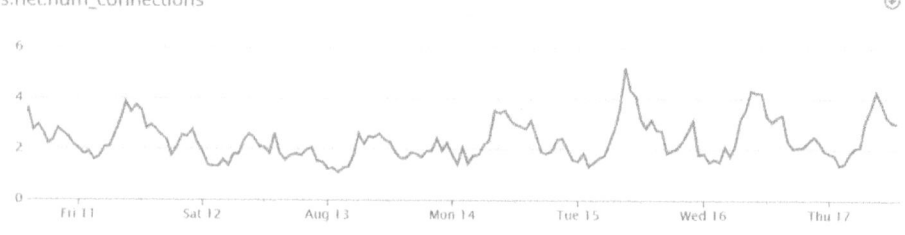

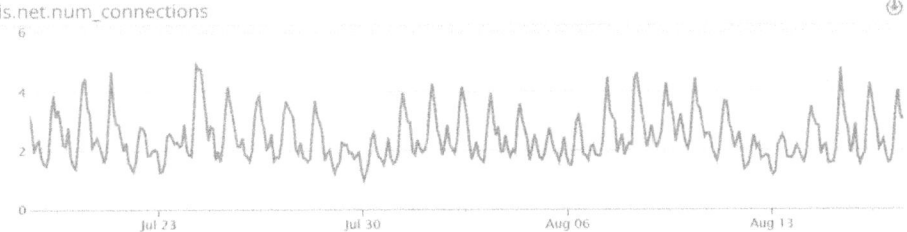

iis.net.num_connections

A good dashboard will often mix several one-hour charts with a few longer timescales that help contextualise the data to the trends, and you can use correlation lines to compare the different resolutions.

Correlation Lines

When this feature is available, the tools will often add correlation lines to all charts on a dashboard to help you see the same time on all charts. This helps to highlight the difference, and is invaluable when investigating an incident.

Correlation Lines

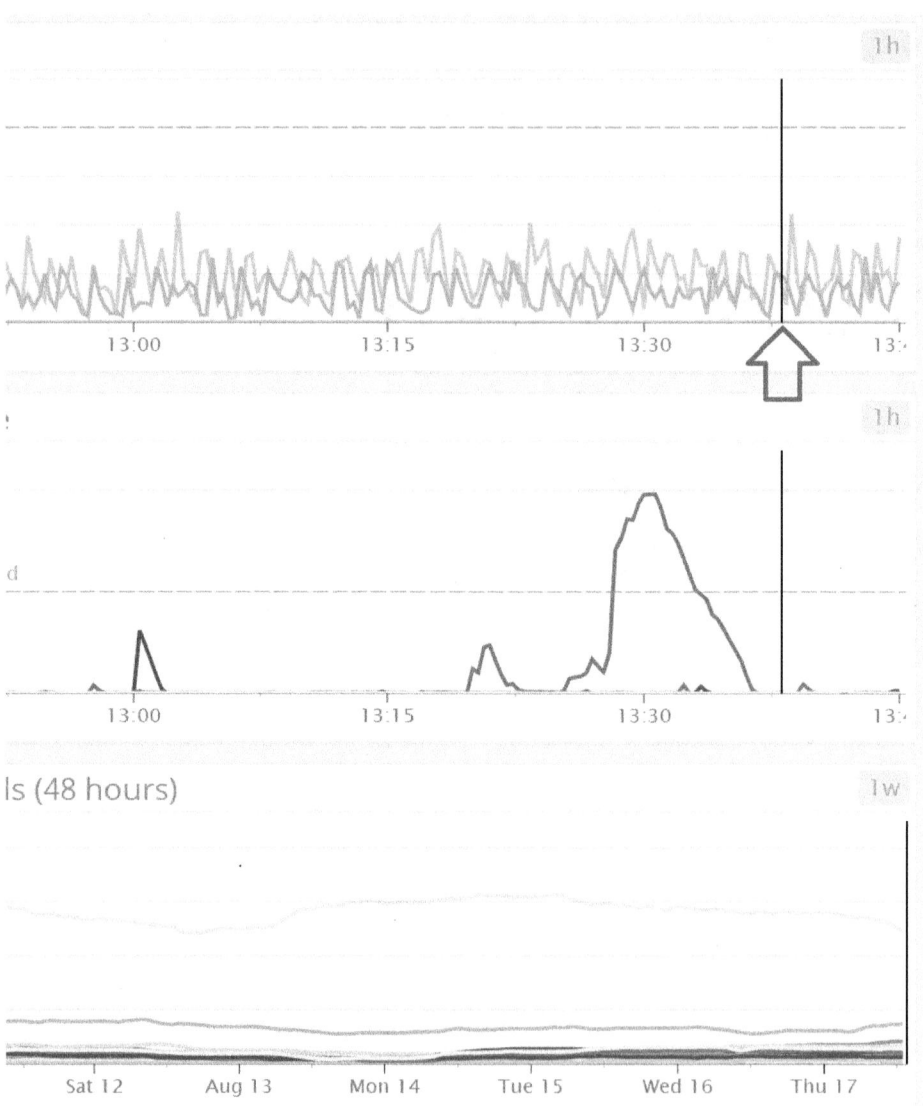

All the vertical correlation lines above represent the same moment in time, even though two of the charts show the last one hour, and one shows the past week.

Integration Dashboards

When investigating an incident, the integration dashboards provide out-of-the-box specialist views over your data. They also supply ideas for charts that you may want to add to your everyday dashboards.

Please note, the screen shots for the dashboards are just to give you a flavour of the out-of-the-box information. They are zoomed out and aren't intended for detailed inspection.

Disk I/O

A collection of metrics for disk operations, including read and write speed, latency, and waits. When you have inexplicable performance problems, or your hosting provider calls you to say you are using too much disk, this is the place to start your investigation.

Disk I/O Dashboard

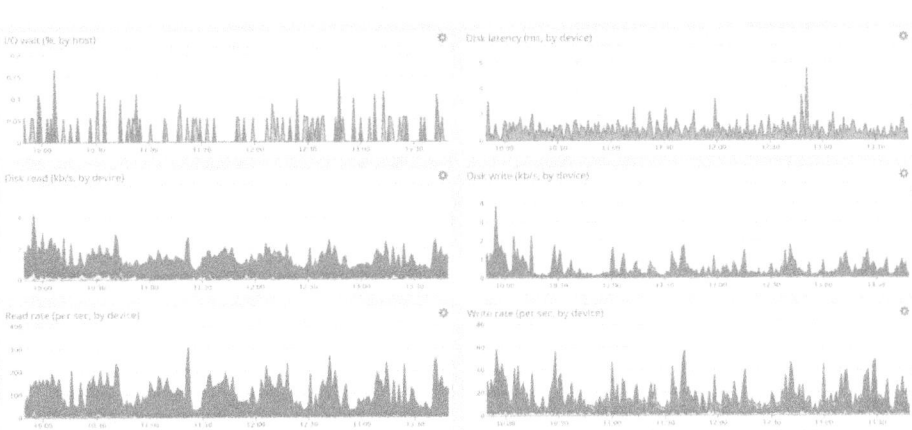

Network

The network dashboard shows ingress and egress traffic, including a per host breakdown. When your network is highly utilised, you can use this dashboard to identify any host that is taking unusually large shares of the network bandwidth.

Network Dashboard

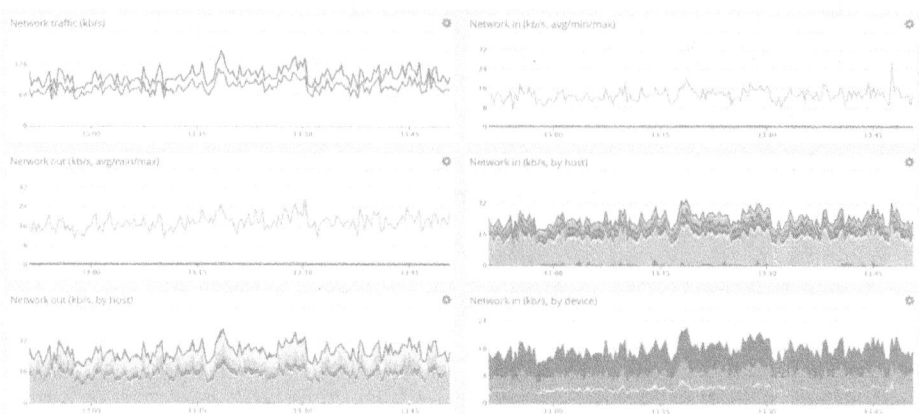

HAProxy

If you were going to create a custom dashboard for HAProxy, it would look exactly like the one you get for no effort. Not only can you see all the important data, you can filter it per service or per backend. You can see many common problem scenarios on this dashboard.

HAProxy Dashboard

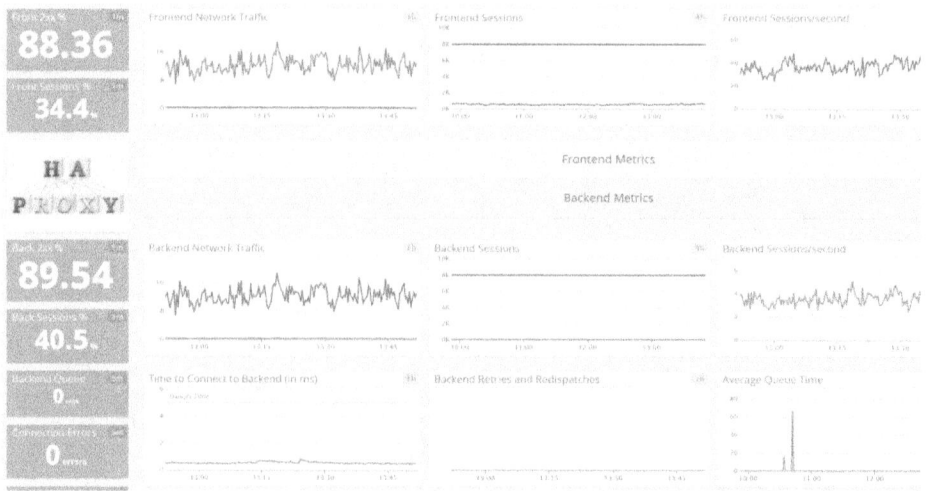

SQL Server

While the SQL Server dashboard isn't as exciting as the HAProxy dashboard, once again it contains a strong set of charts that will help you investigate problems. You can check here that you're getting most of your data from the cache, how many connections you have, and an overview of compilations and blocks. Many of the SQL charts would benefit from markers that show the normal behaviours of your system.

SQL Server Dashboard

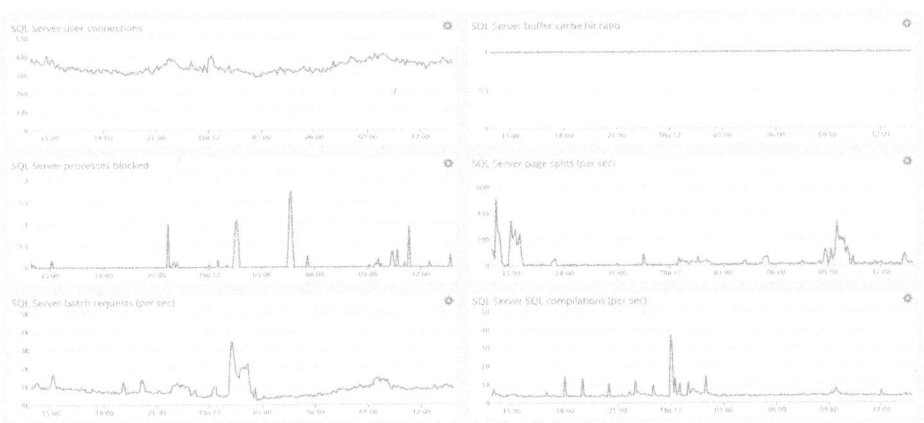

IIS

Once again, the IIS dashboard has everything you need to investigate problems, including the number of requests and connections, which are two common leading metrics for incidents. Just like the SQL metrics, many of these charts would benefit from your markers, so if they are useful add them to your custom dashboard and add marker lines.

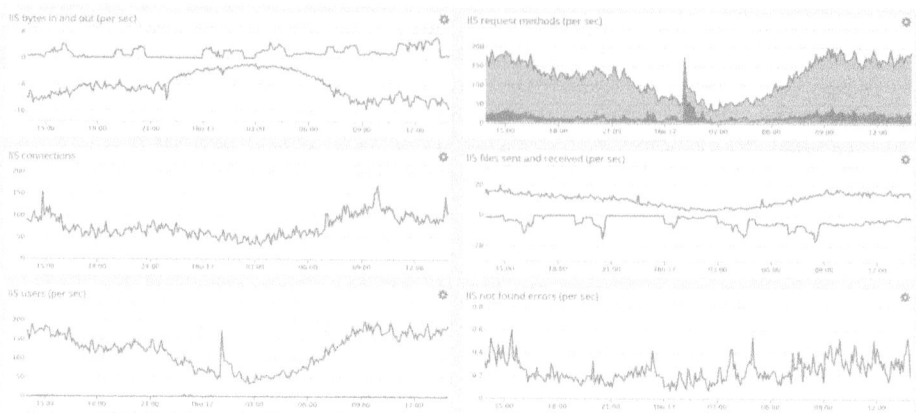

Summary

Each time you add an integration to Datadog, you'll get a standard dashboard that tracks that area. These dashboards are good for incident management, and for generating ideas for metrics that may add value to your everyday dashboards. If you promote a metric to a custom dashboard, consider changing the chart type, splitting the metrics out per host, and adding markers to make the charts more expressive of your context.

You can also use the metric explorer to experiment with the visualisation of a metric, after which you can add it to your custom dashboards. The metric explorer is a good sandbox for these experiments, you can try different settings without worrying about ruining your actual dashboards.

Monitoring and Alerting

When it comes to monitoring and alerting, there is a very fine balance to be struck. Just adding a series of broad brush monitors with default alarms may make you feel warm and fluffy, but it is a strategy that leads to a poor set up that will lead to numerous problems. When you get too many alarms, they lose their importance. If an alarm sounds and it doesn't make you immediately stop what you are doing to investigate, you have alert fatigue. This is a surprisingly common problem. If you get many alerts each day, but none of them are urgent; you need to change the parameters of the alarms.

"Non-urgent alerts" should be moved from your monitoring and alerting into your everyday dashboard. This makes problems visible in a non-urgent way and it won't erode your responsiveness to the information.

Monitor Selection Principles

Your monitoring and alerting strategy should follow this pattern:

1. Pick one metric that is a leading indicator of a fault

2. Add a monitor with a reasonably sensitive alarm threshold

3. Each time the alarm goes off decide whether you need to

   a. Take urgent action to resolve a fault, or

   b. Move the alarm threshold up to make the alarm less likely to sound

It is important to note that you must choose either option a, or option b. There is no option c "ignore the alarm and don't update the alerting". You are on a quest to find the sweet spot where the alarm will sound when there is a problem, with the minimum number of false alarms. Let's quickly revisit the alerting principles:

1. The alarm **MUST** sound if there is a genuine problem
2. The alarm *SHOULD* **NOT** sound unless there is a problem

Once you have hit a good balance with your first monitor, you can use failure events and near-misses to guide your next monitor. Just repeat the pattern of picking a metric that seems related to a fault and adjusting the threshold to achieve the desired result.

Starter Pack

Here are some suggestions of common monitors that you may want to try. Remember to adjust these monitors and alarms based on the above principles.

- No Data: raise a notification if a collection agent stops forwarding data to the platform for more than 5 minutes

- Disk Space: raise a disk space alarm if system.disk.in_use on any device, on any host, is above 0.85 on average for 5 minutes

- CPU: raise a hot-CPU alarm if system.cpu.idle drops below 5% on any host for 15 minutes

- HTTP Check: raise an alarm if an HTTP endpoint is unavailable for 2 minutes

This is a very bare set of monitors and you'll certainly grow this list as part of your incident management process. Introduce your monitors gradually and spend some time fine-tuning them before you move on to adding the next one. Fewer well crafter monitors will be more useful to you than many hastily created ones.

Monitor Categories

There are two handy cheese-slicers you can use to think about different monitors: character and extent.

Here are the characterisations:

- **Availability**: a binary description of whether something seems switched on or off

- **Utilisation**: what percentage of the resource is used, or the size of the item

- **Performance**: how quickly does something respond, is there latency

And here are the various kinds:

- **Network**: bandwidth, packets

- **Server**: CPU, memory, I/O

- **Operating** System: processes, swapping, database

- **Middleware**: web server, message broker

- **Software**: your application

- **Experience**: business metrics, user transactions

You can overlay these two concepts in a monitor matrix.

Monitor Matrix

	Availability	Utilisation	Performance
Network			
Server			
Operating System			
Middleware			
Software			
Experience			

Each of the slots on the matrix has super-powers to find various kinds of problem. If they can find the same root cause, each will do so at different speeds – and you will be able to find circumstances where each one can be the leading indicator when something has broken.

Creating Monitors

This is the part of the book that answers one of the first questions I had about web operations: what should I monitor? Although it is tempting to monitor everything straight away, I'm going to give you a very small number of general monitors. I will also give you a technique for identifying and adding more monitors.

With your knowledge of dashboards, adding a monitor will be simple. You can pick one or more metrics and set conditions that forewarn of problems. When you view a monitor, it shows a chart of the pertinent metrics, overlaid with warning and error bands. This is useful for tuning a monitor, which we'll discuss shortly.

Monitor Summary View

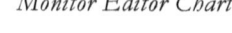

	VALUES	UPTIME
	89.79	100.0 %
	35.02	100.0 %
	89.34	100.0 %
	91.28	100.0 %
	79.03	100.0 %
	92	100.0 %
	57.89	100.0 %
	92.85	100.0 %
	99.83	100.0 %
	67.16	100.0 %

When adding or editing a monitor, the chart can be used to help inform your configuration of the monitor's parameters.

Monitor Editor Chart

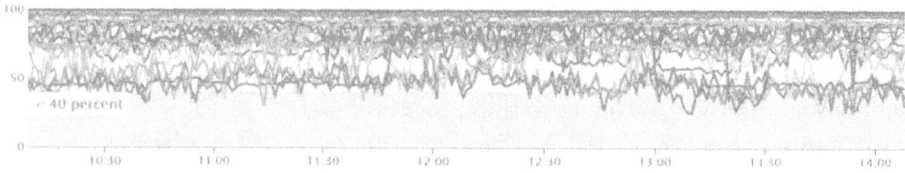

Setting up a monitor is a simple five-step process:

1. Choose a detection method

2. Define the metric
3. Set alarm conditions
4. Set up a description
5. Set up notifications

During the first three steps, the chart will be updated to show you the impact of your changes.

Detection Methods

Although the common method of raising an alarm is a simple threshold (when the disk is 80% full), there are three other methods of detecting a problem. Here is a quick description of each detection method:

- **Threshold**: an alarm is raised whenever a metric crosses a threshold

- **Change**: an alarm is raised when the value of a change is above a threshold

- **Anomaly**: an alarm is raised when some metric moves from an expected pattern by a set number of standard deviations

- **Outlier**: an alarm is raised when a member of a group has different behaviour to the rest of the group based on the selected algorithm

The threshold and change detections are reasonably easy to comprehend. They both trigger an alarm using a number. Threshold uses the current value and change compares the metric over time.

Anomaly detection is slightly more complex. You can adjust the detection by adjusting the settings and reviewing the chart to see where an alarm would be raised.

Anomaly Detection with Two Deviations

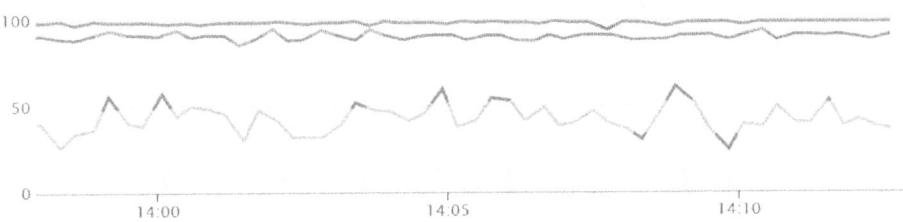

You can adjust the number of deviations and see the effect it has on the chart, increasing the number of deviations reduces the chance of an alarm.

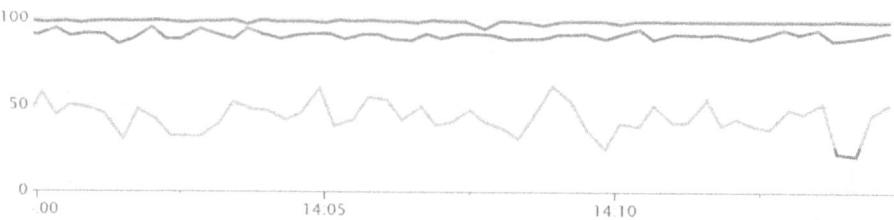

Outlier detection finds members of the monitor group that are behaving differently to the other members. This is a key reason to use good tagging on your hosts as it works best when applied to a group of hosts that you expect to behave in the same way. If you have a mixed group of web servers and database servers, you wouldn't expect their behaviour to be so similar.

Outlier Detection with DBSCAN with Tolerance of 1.5

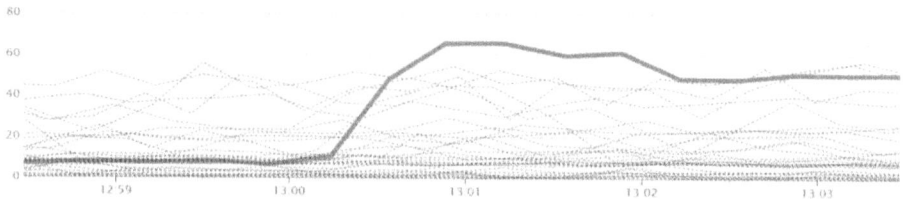

Once again, you can use the preview chart to see the impact of your settings. Normal hosts are shown with a dotted line and abnormal hosts have a solid line. Play with the preview chart to look at different groupings of data using the time series selection options (everything may look fine when looking at the past hour, but try to look at times where you have higher traffic, or when scheduled jobs are running).

The two kinds of algorithm are based on:

- **DBSCAN**: a density based clustering algorithm

- **MAD**: median absolute deviation

When using an algorithm detection method, start with DBSCAN using the default settings and use the monitor selection principles to iterate the configuration of the alarm.

Find out more about DBSCAN here en.wikipedia.org/wiki/DBSCAN and MAD here en.wikipedia.org/wiki/Median_absolute_deviation.

Metrics

In monitoring, metrics refers to the actual data item to monitor and a set of metadata about the conditions to raise an alarm. The elements of the metric differ based on the detection method, but you'll select the metric, and the hosts to include in the monitor before choosing thresholds that put the detection to work.

Experiment with the settings and use the preview chart to predict the impact of your configuration changes.

Alarm Conditions

Alarms can be immediate if a certain condition is met, or require that a condition is present for a certain amount of time before the condition is considered a problem. For example, if you were to raise the alarm every time CPU usage hit 100%, the briefest of CPU spikes will cause alarms to be raised, even though the CPU immediately returns to normal levels. This provides yet another mechanism to iterate your monitors based on the monitor selection principles.

Description

The description contains a message that will be given back to you when a monitor triggers an alarm. You can use this to provide information on the specific details of the alarm, such as the host that has the problem. This is also your chance to remind your future self about why you thought this monitor condition might be worth checking, so include links to your documentation or trouble shooting pages to give yourself a head start. Datadog accepts parameters in the description, so you can insert the specific data, for example the host name and the IP address:

```
The CPU has been more than 95% utilised for fifteen
minutes.

Host: {{host.name}} with IP {{host.ip}}
```

This templating works in the description and the title of the monitor.

Notifications

The notifications section allows you to specify where alerts should be sent. You can send an email, or notify a Slack channel or other integration. You may also integrate with an incident management tool (such as Pager Duty) which can distribute the alarm via SMS, push notifications, or telephone. Don't rely on a single mechanism for your notifications; you are interested in monitoring because you know things go wrong, which means you know that a single notification method can also fail.

Common Monitors

Almost all organisations will monitor and raise alarms for the following items, although the numbers vary based on the infrastructure strategy (i.e. we don't want to hold too many resources in reserve, but we do need a safety margin to act when something changes). The higher your uptime guarantees, the more of everything you'll need to hold in reserve. It is not unusual for a critical network organisation to run with just 20% network utilisation, which makes them highly tolerant to changes in network behaviour.

Metric	Alarm
Disk Space	A disk is more than 80% full.
CPU	A CPU remains above 95% utilisation for more than 10 minutes.
Memory	Memory utilization is above 80% for more than 30 minutes.
Performance	The average HTTP response time is above 200ms for 5 minutes, or if it is above 1,000ms on average for 1 minute.

All the numbers in this table are variables that can be adjusted as part of an experiment to find the right balance of sensitivity. By following the monitor selection principles from the start of this chapter, you will add new metrics and iterate them to get the right balance.

Regularly Reviewing Alarms

Although there are two events that will cause you to review your alarms (a failure you didn't detect, and a false alarm event) – you should also review your alarms regularly. By looking at statistics on a regular basis, you can look for alerting patterns that will reveal areas of improvement.

Datadog has an interactive monitoring report that is great for pattern detection. In the report below, you can see that alarms are commonly generated between midnight and 0100 hours most days. You can also see the top alarms are for low disk space.

This suggests perhaps a backup schedule that pushes the disk space over the alerting threshold most times it runs. Maybe the server should be given additional capacity to ensure the margin of safety is not at risk during these backup runs.

Interactive Monitor Report

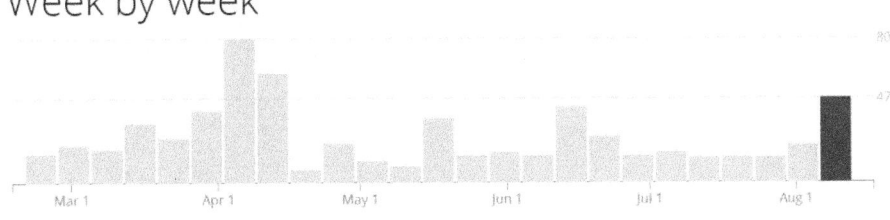

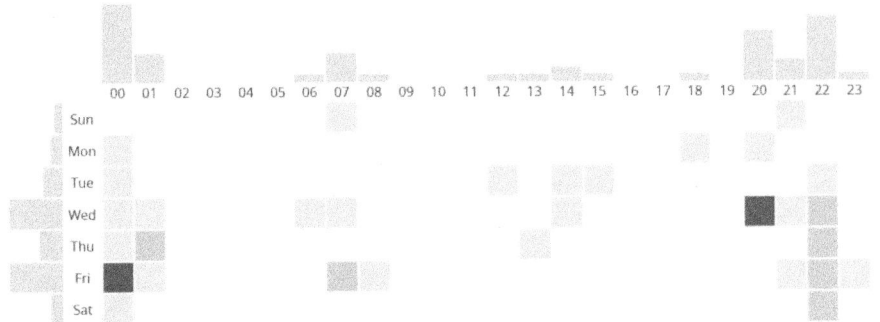

The interactive monitor report can be found at app.datadoghq.com/report/monitor.

Summary

Configuring an awesome set of monitors and alarms is an iterative process that is informed by positive and negative errors in your monitoring configuration. The monitor selection principles guide you to find monitors based on real incidents, and tune their sensitivity to reduce false alarms to the bare minimum.

The Balancing Act

You may have noticed that there are many delicate balancing acts in web operations. Adding the right number of charts to a dashboard is a balancing act between providing plenty of useful data without letting the noise drown the signal. Deciding how much available disk space is a balancing act between paying for disk you don't use, and running out of disk space too quickly before you can act. Handling an incident is a balancing act between taking your time to understand the problem, and resolving the fault quickly.

You may feel that you are the Goldilocks of the DevOps world; but your job is harder. Goldilocks simply solves a false trichotomy each time she is presented with a decision; but you will have to be more precise when you determine how hot or cold your CPUs should be. You can only make the right choice by forming a hypothesis, making an adjustment, and examining the result.

Don't despair though, as if you have implemented a learning culture, failures will guide you towards constantly improving dashboards, monitoring, and alerting.

Cheat Sheet

Monitoring: the process of continually reviewing metrics to detect potential faults, either manually via dashboards or with automated monitors.

Alerting: the process of bringing an automatically detected anomaly to the attention of a human.

The Three Fs

- **Finesse**: arrange for better quality information to be included in the log entry

- **Fix**: fix the underlying problem

- **Filter**: de-classify the log entry so it isn't forwarded to the monitoring platform

Causation Principles

1. Find correlations
2. Arrange everything in the correct order
3. Form a falsifiable hypothesis
4. Test the hypothesis

Monitor Selection Principles

1. Pick one metric that is a leading indicator of a fault

2. Add a monitor with a reasonably sensitive alarm threshold

3. Each time the alarm goes off decide whether you need to

   a. Take urgent action to resolve a fault, or

   b. Move the alarm threshold up to make the alarm less likely to sound

Alerting Principles

1. The alarm **MUST** sound if there is a genuine problem
2. The alarm *SHOULD* **NOT** sound unless there is a problem

Monitor Matrix

	Availability	Utilisation	Performance
Network			
Server			
Operating System			
Middleware			
Software			
Experience			

Acknowledgements

Tony Jones supplied a great deal of sage advice when I was first tasked with configuring web operations monitoring. His advice was the elastic band that turned me into a web operations projectile in my organisation, even though I was a programmer.

I must tip my hat to the detailed work of John Allspaw and Jesse Robbins, whose book Web Operations: Keeping the Data on Time is the definitive work on the subject. I don't cover the same territory so you should get a copy of their book and install its wisdom on your wetware.

My web operations journey was ably supported by a smart software development team. I would like to thank Rachel Green, Ravi Vattikuti, Richard Pargeter, Dhini Hariharan, Madhumita Ghosh-Ray, Silvia Bartolini, Dan Horrocks-Burgess, Jamie Wright, Tudor Williams, and Chris Reay for their support in the implementation of web operations monitoring. I would also like to thank Ian Crickmore for being the communications manager to my incident manager.

I used the LinkedIn recommendations of Shaun Dodimead and Martin Milsom, two colleagues that I would love to work with again one day. If you get the chance to work with either of these people; I can recommend you take it, as they are good humans.

I also need to thank my support network once again for tolerating the highs and lows of making another book; Rebecca and Lily have both supported me by listening to my ideas in their raw, barely intelligible form – and in giving me time and space to write. Dan Horrocks-Burgess once again provided lots of excellent feedback on the early drafts of this book. Any mistakes that remain were inserted maliciously by me after his reviews.

www.ingramcontent.com/pod-product-compliance
Lightning Source LLC
Chambersburg PA
CBHW070104210526
45170CB00012B/743